# No-Cook Cookbook

# No-Cook Cookbook

## Susie Theodorou

Photography by Alex Lau
Creative Direction by Michele Outland
Drawings by Heather Chontos

*Hardie Grant*
NORTH AMERICA

# Grains & Pulses

# Cheese

# Something to Finish

# Suggested Menus

# Introduction

Across the world, so many of us have become food enthusiasts—with a solid interest in and knowledge of great food. We're no longer willing to settle for meals that aren't varied, delicious, and beautiful. And yet, we don't always have the time to cook what we'd like to eat or serve to our loved ones. This is why I came up with the *No-Cook Cookbook*. I wanted to show how easy meals can be assembled quickly and meet our culinary standards.

As a food writer and stylist, I often work with commercial, everyday supermarket products and restaurants that give me an insight into food trends. I love to cook and eat good food. Even after working more than ten hours most days, I still go home and put together a gorgeous meal for myself. Sure, I'm tired, but I have shortcuts for how to make satisfying meals that are quick and where flavor is still at the top of my list. I just have one small rule I follow: combine fresh ingredients with good-quality store-bought products.

You'll love to eat so many of the recipes in this book while simultaneously seeing that they take almost no effort to put together. Combining great flavors to produce remarkable results will start to come naturally to you. This book doesn't just give you recipes—it gives you the fundamentals for how to assemble effortless meals.

I grew up with working parents. From the age of eleven, I would start the family dinner while my mum was on her way home (my dad had no hand in preparing dinner!). I'd wash the salad ingredients, peel the potatoes, joint the chicken (I didn't love this latter task, but I put on a pair of dishwashing gloves, and just did it on chicken Tuesday). I would season the pork chops, and once I got the phone call that my parents were on their way, I would start to cook them. These were simple family meals, but always fresh and using our Greek pantry ingredients.

The memory of those family dinners is ingrained in me and informs how I approach home cooking, even though my meals tend to be much more varied in terms of flavors, techniques, and ingredients. Slowly I have been fine-tuning my "no-cook approach" for food prep on work nights and sometimes on the weekend! Basically, I just assemble!

Over the years, I've seen the trend of salad and grain bowls grow. Travel, magazine, and cookbook projects have shown me how global ingredients have integrated into our everyday cooking, and how the use of plant-based proteins and condiments now play a big role in how we eat.

Flavors have expanded in recent years and procuring global ingredients has become much easier. Mainstream supermarkets stock ingredients like hummus, Asian condiments, and varied international produce. In cities and even some small towns, you can find South Asian, Mediterranean, Middle Eastern, and Asian specialty markets, offering the opportunity to make simple meals with unique bursts of flavor, such as preserved lemons, pomegranate molasses, garlic chili crisp, and more.

It's not just the flavors that have changed but our style of eating and entertaining. The plate is no longer anchored by meat and then rounded out with two to three sides and bread. The plate is now as varied as the global influences. Sometimes it's not even a plate anymore but a bowl or a board—like you see with salad/grain bowls and charcuterie, fish, and cheese boards. And yes, sometimes we do go back to the old plate, but the key is to bring together interesting, fresh flavors that excite both the palate and the eye.

I think of the recipes in this book as meal kits that already exist in most of our kitchens—ones where we take pantry staples and only need to add a few fresh ingredients. I want this book to help you use those staples, both fresh and store-bought, over and over again, until you develop a rhythm and trust in creating your own favorite combinations. You'll start to notice these shortcut ingredients throughout the grocery store. I'm not talking about the prepped chopped salad ingredients but the long-shelf-life staples to have at hand in the pantry and refrigerator—cooked grains in pouches, tins, as well as smoked fish and cured meats.

The first chapter is designed to guide you with easy "measurements" to follow—as simple as a handful of this or that. There are recommendations for what I have labeled as "flavor game changer" ingredients to shop for and keep on hand. And I've suggested kitchen equipment to make the process of assembling dishes easier. From there, the remaining chapters concentrate on no-cook protein ingredients. All the recipes are photographed, even the variations, so you can start to see how making things look good can add no extra time. Some recipes use only three ingredients.

Every chapter includes tips on preparing meals that don't require you to stay in the kitchen but instead allow you to assemble and then hang out. These recipes let you relax, whether it's at the end of your workday or when connecting with loved ones over shared dinners. And the final chapter is dedicated to fun sweet combinations and last bites.

Even though this book was not initially thought of as a book for entertaining, the whole grazing aspect means that there are many dishes that can be shared. As such, I've come up with easy menus to serve on social occasions, whether it's a sports or game night or, hosting out-of-town guests, or book clubs and dates.

No-cook meals mean less time in the kitchen and more time to enjoy life's simple pleasures.

# Pantry Essentials

*Flavor Game Changers*

This chapter is about the foods I love for their flavor, ease of use, and their availability. They feature flavors and textures I regularly combine in all manner of fast, fuss-free, no-cook meals, and hearty snacks. Primarily, this means store-bought oils, vinegars, spices, salad dressings/condiments, and proteins you enjoy. They might be in the dry cupboard, the refrigerator, or the freezer.

You don't have to have all the ingredients listed in this chapter in your pantry at the same time, but being well stocked will expand your options and keep you from making the same things repeatedly. If you use up one ingredient, try replacing it with something different for the sake of variety and a break from routine.

# How To Use This Book

## Weights and Measures

- A cup—make your cup your standard, just don't mix a measuring cup with a tea cup or a mug. If you want to use a home-style cup, stick with that all the time. I grew up with my Greek aunts always using a drinking glass for their measurements.

- A handful of cherry tomatoes is 1 cup/100g.

- An average medium-large heirloom tomato weighs 11½oz/325g; coarsely cut into large pieces for a typical Susie salad, is 2 cups/275g.

- A handful of parsley with stalks is 1oz/30g; handful of leaves is ¾ cup/12g.

- Add a drizzle of extra-virgin olive oil—about ½ Tbsp.; a glug is a good 1 Tbsp. and a bit overflowing.

- One large carrot, weighing 8oz/225g gives you 2 large handfuls of 2-inch/5cm sticks using a julienne peeler, which is 2 cups/175g.

- 1 bunch of Tuscan or curly kale is 8oz/225g (depending where you buy it from!); when the stalks are discarded, and the leaves torn into bite-size pieces it gives 3 large handfuls, is 6 cups/150g. 1 handful of torn kale is 2 cups/50g.

- 1 head of romaine lettuce weighs 12oz/350g. Trimmed and shredded gives 3 heaping handfuls, and is 6 cups/225g. 1 handful is 2 cups/75g.

## Techniques and Why

- When using chopped or sliced raw onions in a recipe, I like to soak them in ice-cold water for 10 minutes then drain them, as it adds a more subtle taste to the recipe with no lingering aftertaste.

- If I do use fresh garlic, I never like to chop it, as it always looks like little teeth in the final recipe. I used to crush it to a paste with salt and the flat side of my knife, but now thanks to the microplane, I grate it to a paste—it takes seconds.

- Smashing cucumbers with a flat side of a chopping knife allows added spices and flavors to penetrate through that thick skin.

- I like to thinly slice or shred crunchy vegetables, garlic, or ginger with a mandoline or julienne peeler, as it allows them to integrate easily with all the other textures in the recipe, be it a grain, shredded cheese, or flaked fish.

Opposite, clockwise from top left: A handful of parsley; shredding crunchy veg with a julienne peeler; red onions soaking in ice-cold water; smashed cucumbers; using the same glass for quick measures; microplane for grating garlic or ginger to a paste.

# Kitchen Equipment Shortlist

The number one tool to have is a good sharp knife, then a couple of other gadgets to perform certain tasks faster and with more precision.

### A SQUIRTY BOTTLE
I do like squirty bottles for my oils, vinegars, and creamy dressings. Now more and more olive oils are being sold in this style of squirty bottle (Graza brand), or they have a spout that pops up when the lid is taken off (Cobram Estate brand).

### MANDOLINE AND MICROPLANE
This OXO white mandoline below is really good. I often use my truffle shaver for slicing veg—I never use it for truffles as they are so expensive, but it's great for Parmesan cheese, radishes, cucumbers, small fennel, zucchini, apples, and pears. (For the microplane see page 10.)

### KITCHEN SCISSORS/SHEARS
I use these for easy-to-snip herbs. They're also good for chicken and other meats when cooking. I prefer my detachable scissors as they can be washed properly.

### VEGETABLE PEELER
I love this simple blade with a rubber handle as it's easy to grip. I also use a julienne peeler for shredding crunchy vegetables (page 10).

**STICK BLENDER**
A lot of the recipes in this book use a stick blender, Vitamix, or food processor. This stick blender takes up very little space in the kitchen and is super efficient.

**SALAD SPINNER**
I do love a salad spinner. I have grown up watching my mum wash all salad leaves and herbs then wait forever for them to drain. I don't have time to wash ingredients 2 hours before I need them. The salad spinner is instant. And they double up as colanders, too.

**LEMON OR LIME SQUEEZER**
I have given in to this gadget as I have had enough of picking out seeds from my dressings.

# The Pantry

I think of pantries as meal kits where you just need to add one or two fresh ingredients to create a no-cook recipe. I want to use what's in my pantry rather than let it fester in the back of the refrigerator or cupboard.

## The Refrigerator

### Fresh veg and salads

This includes salad ingredients like lettuces and kale, and assorted crunchy vegetables such as celery, fennel, radishes, sugar snap peas, snow peas, cucumbers, tomatoes, cabbage (red and green), scallions, and carrots.

### Meats and fish

Think cold cuts (hams and roasted meats from the deli counter), salami and leftover rotisserie chicken. Cured fish such as lox, hot-smoked salmon, mackerel, trout, fresh sushi-grade fish, and fish roe.

### Dairy

Aim to stock a range of cheeses, including hard cheeses—cheddar and Parmesan; semi-hard cheeses like provolone; blue cheeses like Roquefort and Gorgonzola; creamy white cheeses such as ricotta, feta, mozzarella, burrata, goat cheese, and extra creamy Vacherin Mont d'Or, Saint André, Epoisses (a red-rinded soft cheese), and Camembert. Also, keep milk, yogurt, eggs, and butter to hand.

### Tofu and vegan plant-based proteins

All have long refrigerator life.

### Condiments

This category includes store-bought fresh or bottled sauces, dressings, pickles, mayo, and fermented vegetables. Some of these could be perishable and must be kept in the refrigerator (dairy or herb-based dressings or sauces), or they might start in the cupboard but need to be moved to the refrigerator once opened, which I am sure would include mayo. I keep two mayos—Kewpie, an egg yolk base mayo, which lends itself to many Eastern Asian recipes, and a vegan-based mayo (Vegenaise) as I like its extra vinegary flavor.

## The Larder

### Spices and other seasonings

I try to keep only ten of my favorite spices and dried herbs in the cupboard: fennel seeds, sesame seeds (although not a spice or a seed but always in that section in the grocery store!), coriander seeds, ground cinnamon, vanilla extract/bean, Aleppo pepper, sumac, hot pepper flakes, ground cayenne (or other chile) pepper, and dried oregano. Beyond those, kosher salt, flaky Maldon sea salt, and black peppercorns are absolute essentials. Naturally, my basics lean heavily toward Mediterranean cuisines; your culture and personal history will no doubt determine your own favorite basics. The point is to avoid buying every spice under the sun and to try to limit yourself to the ones you use frequently.

### Oils and vinegars

Olive oil (I do have two, one non-virgin that I sauté with, and an extra-virgin oil for salad dressings and for drizzling as a flavorful finish). Toasted sesame oil and chile oil are excellent game changers, adding an extra level of flavor. My vinegars of choice are malt and sherry, and unseasoned rice vinegar and apple cider vinegar are other good basics to have on hand.

### Condiments

Soy sauce, fish sauce, seed and nut butters (tahini, peanut, and/or almond butter), and mayo are other essential bases for making quick dressings or adding a splash of extra flavor for dips.

# Flavor Game Changers

For each of the powerhouses in this list a drizzle, a teaspoon, or a scoop should be all you need to make a big impact on the flavor.

## Chili Crisp or Crunch

*There is a difference!* Chili crisp is a classic Chinese condiment all at once spicy, crunchy, oily, and filled with umami. It has taken on different forms and flavor profiles in recent years; you'll find crunchy jarred versions with varying degrees of garlic and chile from the traditional Sichuan recipe. You will also find chili or garlic crunch, which will usually have the addition of nuts and seeds for that extra texture. These days, you can find Mexican versions of salsa seca (Xilli is my fave or Luchito Crunchy Salsa Macha); there is also White Mausu—a cashew-based chili crunch. Restaurants and grocery stores, including Momofuku and Trader Joe's have their own creations as well. Other brands include Blank Slate (Sichuan chili oil); and big success story—Fly by Jing (Sichuan chili crisp, and xtra spicy chili crisp).

## Crispy fried onions

These are readily available in tubs, pouches, or boxes on the nonperishable shelves in supermarkets. They add immediate texture and flavor to salads.

## Furikake and togarashi

These Japanese seasoning blends are made with nori (seaweed) flakes, black and white sesame seeds, and salt (the furikake in my cupboard is Japanese imported JC Nori Komi furikake). Togarashi is the spicier version with added chile powder (my favorite brand is Holy Tshili). It adds depth of flavor and crunch to salads, tinned, or raw fish recipes and vegetables. Nearly all supermarkets have now developed their own brands.

## Nuts, seeds, and chickpeas

Look for those that are hulled, toasted, or even spiced. Almonds, walnuts, and pecans; sunflower, pumpkin, and sesame seeds; as well as pre-roasted pulses like chickpeas, wasabi peas, and corn. They add interesting flavors and texture sprinkled over a salad or vegetable.

## Pomegranate molasses

This is made by reducing pomegranate juice to a thick syrup. It's a staple of Middle Eastern and Turkish cuisine, and a must in my pantry. The taste is sweet and citrusy with a tart high-end note. Drizzle over yogurt, salads, and crunchy vegetables. I also love it over vanilla ice cream!

## Za'atar

This Middle Eastern staple is made of toasted white and black sesame seeds mixed with dried oregano and thyme. It's excellent sprinkled on salads, yogurts, creamy cheeses, and no-cook protein options. You can find pita and other flatbreads already baked with za'atar as a topping.

## Preserved lemons

These are traditional in Middle Eastern, Mediterranean, and North African cuisines. You use both the rind and flesh. They are made by packing lemons in salt; in the preserving process, the lemons release some of their juice, which combines with the salt to create a salty brine. The lemons pack a powerful punch that's often used to flavor stews; my favorite use is to chop them and add to salsa, hummus, and salads of all kinds.

## Calabrian Chili Paste

These Italian chiles are chopped, crushed, or made into a paste. A teaspoon packs a big punch, so use sparingly. Excellent for sandwiches and dressings, complementing cheese, all meats, and fish.

## Crackers, crisp breads, chips, and breads

The options of crackers, crisp breads, and chips are limitless. Gluten-free variations are just as promising as convectional crackers—with added spices, herbs, seeds, and nuts. Crackers, crisp breads, and chips are good standbys for "croutons" on salads. Keep an eye out for Parmesan crisp crackers and bread croutons, as they are both excellent on salads. With breads and rolls, I keep them ready sliced and individually wrapped in the freezer, so I can just use one or two pieces at a time.

## Flavor Game Changers

### Crunchy vegetable condiments

Pickled vegetables go hand in hand with cured or preserved meats, fish, and cheese, adding crunch and sometimes heat, and always providing acidic notes that complement the proteins. As a bonus, the variety of pickles on grocers' shelves is truly endless. I especially love to keep bread and butter pickles, half sour cucumbers, and pickled okra and green beans on hand. Fermented Asian pickles boast more mellow, sour flavors—these could be carrots, lotus root, cucumbers, daikon, and burdock. Plus preserved vegetable jams (for homemade pickles, see page 21).

### Sriracha

I nearly forgot to add this chili garlic sauce, as it seems to have become an everyday go-to for that extra zap in flavor for sandwiches, avocado toast, and eggs.

### Black garlic

Also known as fermented garlic, this is slowly cooked or dried until the cloves are soft and blackened, and the skin turns a toasted brown. Its origins are from East Asian cooking. You will find it in the vegetable section, loose or in tubs in supermarkets, specialist food shops specializing in spices and herbs, or in Japanese grocery stores. It tastes caramelized, smoky, and earthy all at the same time. You can spread it directly onto crackers or bread; I prefer to use it in a variety of dressings, often replacing fresh garlic.

### Dukkah

A Middle Eastern spice blend, with toasted nuts mixed in with the seasonings. Dukkah can be pistachio-, hazelnut-, or almond-based, with coriander and cumin seeds, sesame seeds, and/or fennel seeds lightly smashed. Some varieties have crushed dried rose petals, too. I like to sprinkle dukkah over fish, chicken, eggs, creamy cheeses, and yogurts. You can simply mix with extra-virgin olive oil and serve as a dip for bread and vegetables.

### Tajin

This is a Mexican spice blend with ground chiles, salt, and a citrus-end flavor (thanks to a high dose of lime). It helps to pep up the flavor of cut fruit, cucumbers, seafood, or even ice cream or shake drinks.

### Fish roe

Salmon roe are fresh, large-ish orange balls (compared to the small flying-fish roe also known as tobiko), with a smoky, salty, subtle-sweet taste. Each gives an individual burst of texture and flavor when bitten, and in my opinion, they add "happiness" to a dish. Flying-fish roe are sometimes infused with wasabi.

## Pantry Proteins

### Pulses and grains

Cans, jars, and pouches of pulses and grains. I find jarred chickpeas, white beans (cannellini), borlotti, and black beans far superior to canned and pouch options, but they do cost more. The pouch options of cooked grains are amazing for me and a revelation at how easy and fast they are to use as their natural flavor and texture are not compromised (page 136).

### Tinned or jarred fish

Aim to stock any combination of tuna, sardines, mackerel, oysters, mussels, and octopus. I used to think that jarred fish was better than tinned varieties, but I now stand corrected on this. The tinned fish are just as tasty. It's important to seek out quality brands that opt for line-caught fish (page 60).

# Fermentation or Pickling

The difference between pickled and fermented vegetables is that pickles are made with acidic ingredients, while the fermented ones are acid-free; the sour flavor is produced from the vegetables sitting in salt.

## Soy-Fermented Boiled Eggs

Mix **4 Tbsp. soy sauce**, tamari, or shoyu with **1¾ cups/400ml unsweetened clear apple juice or water**, **a 2 x 2-inch/5 x 5cm piece of dried kombu (seaweed)**, and a good pinch of **salt**. Bring a small pot of water to a boil, ease **6 large eggs** into the water and boil for 7 minutes (the eggs will be jammy; 8 minutes for hard-boiled). Drain and soak in cold water until cool enough to handle and peel. Ease the eggs into a clean jar with the soy brine. Leave for 1 hour before serving or chill for up to 1 week. Makes 2 cups/500ml

**PREP TIP**
Here the brine is kept cold, so the vegetables retain their color and crunch. Hot brines generally soften the vegetables quickly, taking away that crunch and brightness.

## Super Simple 10-Minute Pickles

Mix ½ cup/120ml **unseasoned rice vinegar** (or red wine vinegar, apple cider vinegar, or malt vinegar) with ¼ cup/60ml water, **2 Tbsp. sugar**, **1 tsp. kosher salt**, and stir to dissolve. Add **2 to 3 handfuls of vegetables** of your choice: peeled shaved beets, carrot sticks or slices, daikon sticks, sliced radishes, sliced cucumbers, sliced red onions or shallots, Asian pears or apple sticks, sliced cauliflower florets. Leave for at least 10 minutes before using. Store in the brine in the refrigerator for a week. Makes 1 cup/250ml

# The Dressings

These dressings are used repeatedly throughout the book. If you have your favorite store-bought variety, feel free to use that. One of my favorite brands is Side-Dish (Getsidedish.com).

## Black Garlic Vinaigrette
**MAKES ½ CUP/120ML**

- 2 black garlic cloves, peeled
- ½ tsp. sea salt flakes
- 1 shallot, finely diced
- 2 Tbsp. sherry vinegar or lemon juice
- 4 Tbsp. extra-virgin olive oil
- 1 Tbsp. chopped thyme, parsley, or cilantro

Finely chop or crush the garlic into a paste with the salt. Place in a bowl and mix with the remaining ingredients and herb of your choice.

## Zhoug
**MAKES 1 CUP/250ML**

- 1 jalapeño
- 1 garlic clove, grated on a microplane
- 2 large handfuls cilantro sprigs
- 1 tsp. each ground cumin and coriander
- ½ tsp. ground cardamom
- 1 tsp. hot pepper flakes
- 5 Tbsp. extra-virgin olive oil
- Juice of 1 lemon
- Sea salt flakes and black pepper

Whizz all the ingredients in a Vitamix, blender, food processor, or use a stick blender. Taste, adding extra lemon juice. Season to taste with salt and pepper. Also good as a dip.

## Mustard Vinaigrette
**MAKES ⅔ CUP/150ML**

- 1 heaping tsp. Dijon mustard
- Tiny amount maple syrup or honey
- 2 Tbsp. finely chopped shallot (from ½ shallot)
- 2 Tbsp. sherry or apple cider vinegar
- 6 Tbsp. extra-virgin olive oil
- Sea salt flakes and black pepper

Mix all the ingredients together in a screw-top jar or whisk with a fork in a small bowl. Adjust seasoning if needed.

## Buttermilk-Style or Ranch
**MAKES 1 CUP/250ML**

- ¾ cup/175ml buttermilk
- 4 Tbsp. extra-virgin olive oil or mayo (depending on how thick you want the dressing)
- 2 anchovies, mashed (optional)
- 3 Tbsp. sherry vinegar
- 1 pinch of sugar
- Sea salt flakes and black pepper
- 2 garlic cloves, grated on a microplane

Mix all the ingredients together in a bowl with a whisk.

## Creamy Peanut Butter and Soy Sauce
**MAKES ½ CUP/120ML**

- 2 Tbsp. smooth or crunchy peanut butter
- 1 Tbsp. soy or fish sauce
- 2 Tbsp. apple juice or water
- 3 Tbsp. light oil, such as sunflower
- 1 Tbsp. toasted sesame oil
- Juice of 1 lime
- 1 tsp. chili oil (optional)

Whisk all the ingredients until well-mixed. Alternative nut butters can be used, such as cashew or almond.

## Green Goddess
**MAKES ½ CUP/120ML**

- 1 tightly packed cup/60g mixed chopped herbs such as chives, parsley, cilantro, tarragon, dill or chervil
- 1 Tbsp. buttermilk or milk
- ½ cup/120ml mayo of choice
- 1 Tbsp. lemon juice
- Sea salt flakes and black pepper

Put all the herbs into a Vitamix, food processor, or use a stick blender. Add the buttermilk and mayo and whizz until smooth and the herbs are well blended in. Taste, season with salt and pepper and a squeeze of lemon juice. Whizz once more.

**Opposite: Black Garlic Vinaigrette**

### Creamy Sesame
**MAKES ½ CUP/120ML**

1½ Tbsp. white miso

1 Tbsp. Japanese sesame paste

1 Tbsp. fresh ginger juice

2 tsp. rice vinegar

2 Tbsp. tamari sauce

Juice of ½ lime

1 pinch of cayenne pepper

5 Tbsp. pineapple (ideally) or apple juice

2 Tbsp. toasted sesame oil

Sea salt flakes

Process all the ingredients together using a stick blender or whisk until smooth and well blended. Taste and adjust the seasoning with salt.

### Tahini Dressing
**MAKES ½ CUP/120ML**

3 Tbsp. tahini paste

Juice of ½ lemon

2 Tbsp. extra-virgin olive oil

Sea salt flakes

Flavor options: 1 Tbsp. chopped preserved lemon, or 1 Tbsp. chopped garlic, grated on a microplane, or 1 tsp. Calabrian chili paste

Mix the tahini with 5 Tbsp. water first. It is essential that it is done this way round. Add the lemon juice followed by the oil. If adding preserved lemons, garlic, or Calabrian chili paste, add these first before adding salt to taste.

### Salsa Verde
**MAKES 1½ CUPS/375ML**

2 Tbsp. each of finely chopped parsley, cilantro, chives, and dill (1 cup/60g in total)

1 tsp. finely chopped rosemary

1 shallot, finely diced

2 Tbsp. sherry vinegar

1 Tbsp. pomegranate molasses

2 Tbsp. coarsely chopped green olives or capers in brine, drained

½ cup/120ml extra-virgin olive oil

1 tsp. toasted sesame oil (optional)

Place all the herbs and shallot in a mixing bowl and stir in the vinegar, pomegranate molasses, olives or capers, and both oils. Taste and adjust seasoning, if needed.

### Avocado and Yogurt Dressing
**MAKES 1 CUP/250ML**

1 large or 2 small ripe avocados, halved, pitted, and peeled

Juice of ½ lemon

3 heaping Tbsp. thick Greek yogurt

1 Tbsp. toasted sesame oil

Sea salt flakes

Hot sauce to taste (optional)

Add all the ingredients to a Vitamix or use a stick blender and process until super-smooth. Season to taste with salt and hot sauce (if using). Can also be served as a dip.

### Avocado and Tomatillo Salsa
**MAKES 1 CUP/250ML**

1 to 2 ripe avocados, depending on size, pitted and peeled

2 to 3 tomatillos, depending on size, husks removed

1 big handful cilantro

1 jalapeño, or a few drops hot sauce like habanero sauce

Juice of 1 lime

½ white onion, coarsely chopped

2 tsp. toasted sesame oil

Sea salt flakes

Add all the ingredients to a Vitamix or use a stick blender and process until super-smooth, about 2 minutes. Season to taste with salt and add extra lime juice, if needed. Also good as a dip.

### Avocado and Cucumber
**MAKES 1½ CUPS/375ML**

1 English cucumber, peeled, halved lengthwise, and seeded

1 large ripe avocado, halved, pitted, and peeled

3 Tbsp. avocado or extra-virgin olive oil

1 heaping Tbsp. pickled jalapeños

Juice of 1 to 2 limes

Sea salt flakes and black pepper

Add all the ingredients, except the lime juice, to a Vitamix, food processor or use a stick blender and process until super-smooth. Taste. Add enough lime juice to taste and some salt and pepper. Whizz once more. Serve. This is also good as a dip.

**Opposite: Salsa Verde**

# Rotisserie Chicken

*The Perfect Ingredient*

A rotisserie chicken offers the cook the chance to assemble a hot meal without ever having to turn on the stove or oven. This chapter teaches you to carve and cut the chicken for a whole variety of recipes. There are big salads to serve with the ubiquitous rotisserie chicken, coleslaws, and variations on the classic mayo-based "American" chicken salad, as well as sandwiches and quick three-ingredient ideas you can put together for your satisfying chicken meal every time.

Even though rotisserie chicken was available from the early 90s in the USA, in the last couple of decades we have seen the quality of the rotisserie chicken market expand more than ever. These days, the birds are not only available in upmarket specialist food stores but every supermarket. And now, the birds are also prepared with different seasonings and packed with different flavor profiles, all helping to make meals more interesting and varied.

## PREP TIPS

- As well as the whole bird, more and more supermarkets are selling the chicken portioned in halves and quarters, so if you are preparing for one or two, you don't have to eat the chicken all week!

- Choose a rotisserie chicken from the supermarket that is still very hot and juicy in the bag, to guarantee freshness.

- Try to always serve the chicken with fresh leafy salads, coleslaw, or quick grains for a complete meal.

- 1 (2lb/900g) rotisserie chicken will serve four people; bones removed, it gives 1lb/450g/4 cups chicken meat, shredded or sliced.

Clockwise from top left: Crispy tostadas; leafy salad; store-bought giardiniera—conventional and spicy hot; portioned rotisserie chicken; sauces to serve with rotisserie chicken—Avocado and Yogurt (page 24), Zhoug (page 23), and Spicy Mayo (page 57).

# Carving the Rotisserie Chicken

The chicken should be carved into six or eight pieces, depending on whether the leg and thigh are separated.

Remove the drumstick and thigh together, by pulling away from the body of the bird and sliding your knife into the joint that's attached to the carcass. Cut.

Place the chicken on a cutting board and remove the elastic used to truss the bird. Make sure your knife is sharp—it really helps.

If liked, you can separate the drumstick from the thigh—just cut through the joint.

**THE CARCASS**
The carcass is the name given to the bone frame of the chicken. Once the meat is removed from the carcass, don't forget to turn the carcass upside down and pull out the juicy, delicious "oysters," near where the thigh was attached—there are two of these. Enjoy.

To remove the breast, cut from the top of the carcass, sliding the knife down the side, staying close to the carcass, and cutting all the time. Repeat on the other side.

**TO SERVE WHITE MEAT**
Cut the chicken breast into about ½-inch-/1cm-thick slices, or cut it into thirds for more substantial pieces, or shred with two forks.

To remove the wing, slide the knife between the joint that attaches the wing drum to the breast, and cut. Repeat on the other side.

**TO SERVE DARK MEAT**
Remove the dark meat from the drumstick: hold the drumstick upside down on the cutting board and cut down to separate the meat from the bone. Cut the meat into slices or shred using two forks.

Remove the meat from the thigh: place the thigh, skin-side down on the board, and slide your knife between the bone and the meat, cutting very close to the bone. Cut the meat into slices or shred using two forks.

# Leafy Salads to Serve with Rotisserie Chicken

It's a good idea to have a couple of salads in your repertoire that work as a side to almost all proteins. For me, it's a seasonal leafy salad and our family Greek chopped salad. One of these salads and coleslaw (on page 34) is all you need for a complete rotisserie chicken meal.

### Mixed Leaf Salad

Use a mixture of lettuce like peppery **radicchio** or **treviso lettuce**, a robust green leaf like **endive**, and a buttery mild leaf like **little gem**. Tear a mixture of these leaves into 1-inch/2.5cm bite-size pieces to give you 4 heaping handfuls. Add to a large bowl and add **2 handfuls of cherry tomatoes**, halved. Dress with ½ cup/120ml dressing such as **Buttermilk-Style (page 23)**, **Mustard Vinaigrette (page 23)**, or **Black Garlic Vinaigrette (page 23)**. Top with a handful of **nasturtiums** and chopped **chives**. Serves 4

## Greek Chopped Salad

In a large bowl, toss 3 cups/225g shredded romaine lettuce, 2 cups/150g shredded iceberg lettuce, 1 cup/135g thinly sliced celery, 2 Persian cucumbers, chopped, 2 ripe tomatoes, chopped, and 1 handful each of cilantro and parsley sprigs, chopped. Drizzle in 3 Tbsp. malt vinegar, 4 Tbsp. extra-virgin olive oil, and season with salt. Toss and taste, adjusting seasoning if necessary. Serves 4

# Four Coleslaws to Serve with Rotisserie Chicken

Coleslaw acts as both salad and a "sauce" for the chicken, as well as adding extra texture with its crunch. It also expands your options on how to serve the chicken: on a plate, in a sandwich, or wrapped in a taco. If in a hurry, use your favorite store-bought coleslaw.

Opposite, clockwise from top left:

## Classic Coleslaw

Soak **1 handful of very thinly sliced red onion** in ice-cold water for 10 minutes. Meanwhile, make a dressing in a large bowl with **1 Tbsp. Dijon mustard, 2 Tbsp. apple cider vinegar, 2 tsp. sugar, ½ cup/ 120ml your favorite mayo, and ½ cup/120ml sour cream or crème fraîche** and mix until smooth. Add **3 big handfuls of shredded green cabbage** and **2 handfuls of carrot sticks.** Drain the onions and add to the other ingredients. Toss well. Season with **sea salt flakes and black pepper.** Makes 1 ½ cups/375ml

## Smoky Carrot and Kale Slaw

In a large bowl, toss **2 handfuls of carrot sticks, 2 handfuls of shredded red cabbage,** soaked and drained, and **1 large handful of torn Tuscan kale leaves.** Mix in **½ cup/120ml Sriracha mayo, 1 tsp. toasted sesame oil,** and **1 Tbsp. toasted sesame seeds.** Season. Makes 2 cups/500ml

## Spicy-Hot Green Coleslaw

Cut **2 scallions** into long strips and soak in ice-cold water for 10 minutes to make them curl. Meanwhile, in a large bowl, mix **2 big handfuls of shredded green cabbage, 1 large handful of torn Tuscan kale leaves, 1 green apple such as Granny Smith,** cut into thin sticks, and **1 serrano chile,** cut into thin sticks. In a small bowl, mix **3 Tbsp. each of mayo** and **sour cream** until smooth. Add to the salad mix, rubbing well with your hands. Taste and season with **sea salt flakes** and **lemon juice.** Drain the scallions and use to top the coleslaw just before serving. Makes 2 cups/500ml

## Red Cabbage and Tahini Slaw

Soak **2 handfuls of thinly sliced red cabbage** in ice-cold water for 10 minutes. This makes the cabbage crisp and stops it making the rest of the ingredients purple! Meanwhile, toss together **1 large handful of shredded carrots, 1 red chile, chopped** (optional) with **1 handful of arugula.** Drain the cabbage and add to the carrot mixture. Add the juice of **½ lemon** and **1 quantity Tahini Dressing (page 24)** and toss well. Taste and adjust the seasoning with **sea salt flakes,** if needed. Lightly mix in **1 handful of cilantro sprigs.** Serve. Makes 1 ½ cups/375ml

# Herbed Beans with Rotisserie Chicken

White beans dressed with little more than fresh herbs and good olive oil reminds me of meals I've enjoyed in Tuscany, the South of France, and the Greek islands. Here, the gremolata-style dressing is inspired by the Italian version made with garlic, citrus rind, and parsley. My variation uses a combination of preserved lemons, black garlic, and cilantro. The black garlic can be replaced with pitted salted olives—not the same, but it does have that "grounding" umami flavor.

**SERVES 4**

- 1 small preserved lemon, halved and seeds discarded
- 1 small black garlic bulb, skin discarded
- 1 handful cilantro or flat-leaf parsley
- 3 Tbsp. extra-virgin olive oil
- Juice of ½ lemon
- 1 pinch of hot pepper flakes
- 2 cans (15oz / 425g each) white beans, chickpeas, or borlotti beans, drained and rinsed
- 1 (2lb / 900g) rotisserie chicken of your choice, carved into 8 pieces or coarsely sliced
- Cilantro sprigs, for serving

Finely chop the lemon, garlic, and cilantro, then mix together with the oil, lemon juice, and hot pepper flakes.

Set aside 2 Tbsp. gremolata and stir the rest into the beans. Taste and adjust the seasoning, if needed. Place the beans on a serving platter and arrange the carved chicken on top. Drizzle with the reserved gremolata and top with cilantro sprigs to serve.

**QUICK SWAP**
You can change up the dressing and toss the beans with Zhoug (a Middle Eastern herb sauce, page 23) or a store-bought pesto of your choice.

# The Chicken Salad Four Ways

Below are four variations on chicken salad. Either serve with little gem lettuce cups, herbs, sliced radishes, pickles, and crackers, or follow any of the serving ideas.

**ALL RECIPES MAKE 1 TO 1½ CUPS/250 TO 375ML CHICKEN SALAD**

### Green Goddess Chicken Wedge Salad

Mix **1 cup/225g shredded chicken**, white, dark, or a mixture, **or 2 chicken breasts (9oz/250g)** cut into ½-inch/1cm chunks and toss with ½ **quantity Green Goddess Dressing (page 23).** Serve 3 to 4 heaping Tbsp. chicken salad over a **large wedge of iceberg lettuce**, accompanied with **crispy onions** and **half sour pickle slices.** Drizzle with a little extra Green Goddess Dressing, if liked.

## Classic Chicken Salad Focaccia Sandwich

In a bowl, mix ½ cup/120ml mayo, 4 Tbsp. sour cream or crème fraîche, and 1 Tbsp. pickle juice from your favorite pickles, such as half sour pickles, until smooth. Add 1 cup/225g shredded chicken, white, dark, or a mixture, or 2 chicken breasts (9oz/250g) cut into ½-inch/1cm chunks, and toss to coat the chicken. Taste and adjust the seasoning with sea salt flakes. Use to make a sandwich with focaccia bread, arugula, sliced tomatoes, sliced red onions, and pickled yellow banana peppers.

## Salsa Verde Chicken Salad with Kale

Place **1 cup/225g shredded chicken, white, dark, or a mixture, or 2 chicken breasts (9oz/250g)** cut into ½-inch/1cm chunks in a large bowl and toss with ½ **quantity of Salsa Verde (page 24)**. To make into a kale salad, toss **1 small handful of torn Tuscan kale leaves, 1 small handful of shaved fennel, ½ heirloom tomato, coarsely chopped,** and **½ medium avocado, coarsely chopped.** Top with **3 to 4 heaping Tbsp. chicken salad,** then serve.

## Kimchi Chicken Wedge Salad

Drain ½ cup/75g red kimchi, (brand of your choice), setting aside 1 Tbsp. kimchi liquid. Chop the kimchi and mix in a large bowl with the reserved liquid, ½ cup/120ml Kewpie mayo, 1 tsp. toasted sesame oil, 1 cup/225g shredded chicken, white, dark, or a mixture, or 2 chicken breasts (9oz/250g) cut into ½-inch/1cm chunks. Taste and adjust seasoning with sea salt flakes. Serve 3 to 4 heaping Tbsp. chicken salad over 1 large wedge iceberg lettuce, topped with sliced radishes and toasted sesame seeds.

# Family Taco Salad Platter

I'm a big fan of Chipotle and Sweetgreen. I ate in this way before either of these food chains came along, mainly due to my Mediterranean background. This all-in-one family salad keeps the components separate so that everyone can choose which parts they prefer to serve themselves. Choose a rotisserie chicken that's been cooked with a spice rub or BBQ sauce.

**SERVES 4**

1 pouch (9oz/250g) white or brown rice

3 Tbsp. finely chopped cilantro

2 Tbsp. extra-virgin olive oil

Sea salt flakes and black pepper

1 can or jar (15oz/425g) black beans, drained and rinsed

2 Tbsp. chopped chipotle peppers in sauce, plus 2 Tbsp. sauce

2 Roma tomatoes, diced

2 Tbsp. diced white onion

1 head (8oz/225g) romaine lettuce, coarsely cut into strips

Juice of 1 lime

1 (2lb/900g) Colombian or BBQ rotisserie chicken, meat sliced or shredded

2 radishes, shaved and soaked in ice-cold water for 10 minutes, drained

Toasted pumpkin seeds, pickled jalapeños, and lime wedges, for topping

1 quantity Avocado and Tomatillo Salsa (page 24) and tortilla chips, for serving

Heat the rice in the microwave for 90 seconds. Empty into a bowl, using a fork, then toss with the cilantro and 1 Tbsp. of the olive oil. Taste and add salt and pepper, if needed.

Mix the beans with the chipotle peppers and sauce. Stir and season to taste. Set aside.

Mix the tomatoes and white onion in a small bowl, and season to taste (this is the pico de gallo).

Place the lettuce on a large serving platter and season with lime juice, the remaining olive oil, salt, and pepper. Mix well. Arrange the chicken and other salad components over the lettuce in piles of two. Scatter the radishes, pumpkin seeds, jalapeños, and limes over the top. Serve with the salsa and tortilla chips.

**QUICK SWAP**
This salad can be made in even less time, as you can buy your favorite seasoned black beans, pico de gallo, and salsa. All you need to do is shred the chicken and lettuce then follow the assembling directions.

# Chicken Tostada Night

A store-bought tostada is a crispy fried corn tortilla. I like the crunchiness of tostadas, but if you prefer soft flour or corn tortillas then that's the way to go. Just toast the tortillas on an open flame or in a cast-iron skillet to get that smoky taste. The number of condiments you provide is up to you—add a pico de gallo, diced cucumbers, thinly sliced radishes crisped in ice-cold water, and grated cotija (or feta) cheese.

**SERVES 4**

### Jicama salad

- 1 small jicama (1lb/450g), quartered and peeled
- 1 ripe mango, peeled and flesh cut away from stone
- Juice of 1 lime, plus extra for the red cabbage
- 4 shakes of Tajin

### Chicken

- 1 (2lb/900g) Colombian or BBQ rotisserie chicken, shredded
- Sea salt flakes and black pepper
- 2 Tbsp. toasted sesame or avocado oil (optional)
- 1 large handful shredded red cabbage, soaked in ice-cold water for 10 minutes, drained
- 8 to 12 tostadas or toasted tortillas
- 1 cup/250ml sour cream
- 1 handful arugula leaves
- ½ cup/50g each of pickled jalapeños and red onions (page 21)
- Lime wedges, for serving

Cut the jicama and mango into 2-inch/5cm long, about ¼-inch/5mm thick sticks. Mix with the lime juice and Tajin. Chill until required.

Place the chicken in a large serving bowl and season with salt and pepper and a little sesame or avocado oil, if liked. The chicken is so well flavored you can probably skip this step.

Season the red cabbage with lime juice, salt, and pepper to taste.

Serve all the components separately for everyone to make their own tostadas—layering in this general order—sour cream, arugula, chicken, cabbage, jicama salad, and pickled jalapeños or red onions. Squeeze lime wedges on top.

# Three-Ingredient Chicken Cheats

These recipe ideas use up leftover rotisserie chicken—just mix the shredded chicken with a jar of your favorite marinated vegetable, pickle, or sauce. The delicatessens of this world are packed floor to ceiling with condiments to choose from.

**ALL RECIPES SERVE 1**

Opposite, clockwise from top left:

## Giardiniera Chicken Baguette

Drain ½ **cup/55g giardiniera vegetables** (the spicy version is really good) and mix with **1 cup/225g shredded chicken**. Drizzle with **olive oil** and season to taste, if needed. Serve in a **soft Italian-style baguette**, brushing the inside of the bread with a little of the brine from the jar of vegetables.

## Zhoug Chicken with Couscous

Mix 1 to 2 Tbsp. **Zhoug** (page 23) with **1 cup/225g shredded chicken** using a fork to keep the mixture light. Serve over **1 cup/230g prepared couscous or grains**.

## Pesto Chicken with Mixed Chicory Salad

Mix **1 cup/225g shredded or diced chicken** with 1 to 2 Tbsp. **pesto of your choice** using a fork to keep the mixture light and to prevent mushiness. Place the pesto chicken over a bowl with **mixed chicories—radicchio, escarole, Belgian salad leaves**—and arugula, about 2 handfuls.

## Wild Marinated Mushrooms and Chicken Bruschetta

A little bit of cooking here is to toast a **thick piece of sourdough bread**, or if super fresh, serve as is. Place the bread on a plate. Mix **2 heaping Tbsp. marinated mushrooms** with **1 cup/225g shredded chicken**. Scoop onto the toast and drizzle with a little more of the **mushroom oil**.

# Chicken Caesar Salad

The lettuce for a Caesar is predetermined to be romaine, but I prefer little gems, so choose your favorite. Baby kale or torn Tuscan kale leaves are also robust enough to be coated in such a thick Caesar dressing. Alternatively, you can use a mix of radicchio, treviso, rosabella radicchio, and Castelfranco when they are all in season during spring.

**SERVES 4**

## Dressing
(makes ⅔ cup/160ml)

- 2 garlic cloves, grated on a microplane
- 3 anchovy fillets or 2 Tbsp. Worcestershire sauce
- 2 Tbsp. white wine vinegar
- 1 heaping tsp. Dijon mustard
- 1 pinch of sugar
  Sea salt flakes and black pepper
- 1 large egg yolk
- 4 Tbsp. sunflower or grapeseed oil
- 4 Tbsp. extra-virgin olive oil

## Salad

- 4 heads little gem lettuce, separated
- 1 cup/70g mandoline-shaved Parmesan cheese (the more cheese the better)
- 8 Parmesan crisp crackers or 20 garlicky croutons
- 1 (2lb/900g) rosemary garlic rotisserie chicken, sliced or shredded

For the dressing, place the garlic in a large bowl, add the anchovies, and mash with the back of a fork into the garlic. Alternatively, stir in the Worcestershire sauce. Stir in the vinegar, mustard, sugar, and some pepper. Whisk in the egg yolk, then start to gradually whisk in both oils until thickened. Taste, adding salt, if needed.

Start to add the salad leaves to the dressing, tossing to coat the leaves in the dressing. Stir in half the Parmesan.

Transfer the leaves to a large serving bowl, or four individual bowls, top with the remaining cheese, and crush the Parmesan crisps on top, Finish with the chicken and more cheese.

**QUICK SWAP**
Either use your favorite ready-made Caesar dressing or 1 cup/250ml mayo, mixed with grated garlic, crushed anchovies or Worcestershire sauce, and vinegar. Mix. Taste, adding salt, if needed.

# Sesame Chicken Salad Bowl

This salad uses spiralized or shredded zucchini. If you have a machine at home, great; or look out for them already prepared in the fresh salad section of grocery stores. Alternatively, you can cut the zucchini into long thin sticks with a julienne hand peeler.

**SERVES 2**

½ quantity Creamy Sesame Dressing (page 24)

2 big handfuls spiralized or julienned zucchini

2 handfuls small salad leaves like baby spinach, arugula, tatsoi, or baby kale

Sea salt flakes and black pepper

Squeeze of lime juice

1 large, thick carrot, peeled and made into julienne strips

1 long green pepper, thinly sliced

1 Persian cucumber, thinly sliced

3 radishes, thinly sliced and soaked in ice-cold water, drained

2 (9oz/250g) rotisserie chicken breasts of your choice, thickly sliced (or use ½ chicken, mixing the dark and white meat slices)

Furikake or toasted sesame seeds and crispy onions, for sprinkling

Use 1 Tbsp. of the dressing to dress the zucchini noodles, then divide the vegetable between two serving bowls.

Lightly dress the salad leaves with a little dressing and a squeeze of lime juice. Season to taste and pile into the salad bowls next to the zucchini. Going around the salad bowl, top with the carrot strips, sliced peppers, cucumber, and radishes.

Top the center of the salads with sliced chicken. Drizzle with the remaining sesame dressing and sprinkle with furikake or whichever crunchy topping you like to use.

**FLAVOR SWAP**
You can use the Creamy Peanut Butter and Soy Dressing (page 23) in place of the sesame, and sprinkle with chopped roasted peanuts (I like them ready salted!).

# Vietnamese Salad with Chicken

I like to use both green and ripe fruit, be it green papaya with ripe mangoes, or green mangoes with ripe mangoes. You can also use carrots for the crunch instead of the green papaya or mango. For flavor, you are aiming for a mix of spicy hot (chiles) and acid (limes), salty (fish or soy sauce), and umami (jerked mushrooms or tofu). This is a brilliant way of using up chicken to make an appetizer or main salad.

**SERVES 4**

**Nuoc Cham Dressing**

- 2 Tbsp. rice wine vinegar
- 1½ Tbsp. fish sauce or soy sauce
- Juice of 1 lime
- 1 Tbsp. sugar
- 1 bird's eye chile—this is super-hot, so seed or use 1 Tbsp. Sriracha (modern addition)

**Salad**

- 3 big handfuls shredded green mango, green papaya, or mixed carrots
- 1 big handful shredded ripe mango
- 2 cups/450g shredded rotisserie chicken, breast and/or brown meat, or whichever you prefer
- 1 small handful each of mint sprigs, Thai basil sprigs, and cilantro sprigs
- 1 handful sliced jerked mushrooms or tofu
- 2 Tbsp. chopped roasted peanuts
- 2 Tbsp. crispy onions
- 1 red chile, thinly sliced (optional)
- Shrimp crackers, for serving (optional)

Mix all the dressing ingredients together in a bowl with ⅓ cup/80ml water and set aside.

Put all the shredded fruits or carrots into a large bowl, toss to mix, then add half of the dressing and toss once more.

Add the chicken to a second bowl and toss with the remaining dressing.

Let both mixtures stand for 10 minutes for the flavors to combine.

To assemble, mix the chicken and fruit together, tossing gently to combine. Add the herbs, leaving a few sprigs behind for the garnish.

Divide the salad between four serving bowls, piling the mixture high in the center of the dish. Top with the jerked mushrooms or tofu, reserved herbs, and finish with the peanuts, crispy onions, chile, and shrimp crackers, if liked.

Note: The dressing is quite watery (all part of its charm), which is why it's best served in a bowl.

This page: Green papaya, halved, seeds scooped out, and peeled.
Opposite: Green papaya shredded into julienne strips using a hand peeler.

# Bahn Mi with BBQ Rotisserie Chicken

Bahn Mi is the classic Vietnamese baguette sandwich with BBQ meat and pickles. The baguette should be fresh and soft and able to soak up all the pickle juices. Choose a BBQ or spicy-hot style of rotisserie chicken for this.

**MAKES 4 SANDWICHES, SERVES 2 TO 4 PEOPLE**

### Pickles

- ½ cup/ 120ml unseasoned rice vinegar
- 2 Tbsp. sugar
- 1 tsp. salt
- 2 big handfuls carrot sticks
- 1 piece (8in/20cm) thick daikon, cut into sticks like the carrot

### Spicy mayo

- ¾ cup/ 175ml mayo of your choice (Kewpie is a good one for here)
- 1½ Tbsp. hot chili sauce, such as Sriracha or sambal oelek
- 2 Tbsp. finely chopped scallions (about 1 thick scallion)
- 2 splashes of tamari, to taste

### Sandwich

- 1 large Persian cucumber or 2 small
- ½ tsp. sea salt flakes
- Chili sesame oil, for drizzling
- 1 long sourdough or classic French baguette, or 2 small baguettes
- ½ (1lb/450g) BBQ rotisserie chicken, sliced or shredded (mix of brown and white meat)
- 1 large handful cilantro sprigs

First, make the pickles. Mix the vinegar, ¼ cup/60ml water, sugar, and salt together in a medium bowl. Mix in the vegetables. Place in the refrigerator to crisp and pickle for 15 minutes, tossing halfway through.

Meanwhile, for the spicy mayo, mix all the ingredients together. Taste and adjust the level of heat, if liked.

For the sandwich, quarter the cucumber lengthwise. Smash with the side of your chopping knife. Sprinkle with the salt and a drizzle of chili sesame oil and let stand for about 5 minutes.

To assemble, cut the baguette in half lengthwise and separate in two. Press the white part of the bread into the crust and spread both sides with spicy mayo. Randomly place pieces of cucumber on the base and top with the chicken. Drain the pickles and press onto the chicken. Place the cilantro sprigs on top. Press down the top part of the baguette to sandwich the filling, and secure with toothpicks in four equal places, or butcher's string. This is to allow even cutting without everything rolling around. Cut the baguette in half, then in half again to make four equal sandwiches. Serve with any remaining spicy mayo and pickles.

**QUICK SWAP**
Feel free to use store-bought spicy mayo. The choice is endless.

# Fish & Shellfish

*Fresh, Tinned, and Smoked*

With fish, no-cook cooking centers on tinned and smoked options, or leaving the freshest catch in its natural state and serving crudo, ceviche, or tartare. Smoked fish—chiefly salmon, mackerel, trout, or white fish—are instant meal makers, in salad or grain bowls and well beyond for meals throughout the day.

The current very fashionable tinned fish—tuna, mackerel, sardines, salmon, and anchovies—are all easily incorporated into dinners, lunches, snacks, and even breakfast. Cooked shellfish from the fish counter (or frozen) provides an excellent foundation for a full meal: shrimp, lobster, and crab are flavorful, versatile partners with vegetables and grains of all sorts.

**PREP TIPS**

- Vacuum-sealed hot-smoked fish from the grocery store keeps very well in the refrigerator; it has at least a six-week shelf-life if unopened.

- Pickles (cucumbers, cornichons, capers, and onions) and peppery leaves such as arugula, endive, radicchio, and escarole are good partners for the rich flavor and texture of smoked fish.

- The best sources for sushi-grade fish are Asian supermarkets, Japanese, Korean H-marts, and other similar markets. Sushi-grade fish may be labeled as fish for sashimi— the fillet has been prepared for you— skinned and boned, ready to be sliced or diced by you.

Clockwise from top: Capers and caper berries; prepping Lox Grain Bowl (page 78); cold-smoked salmon trout; smoked salmon, and lox; sushi-grade fish fillets.

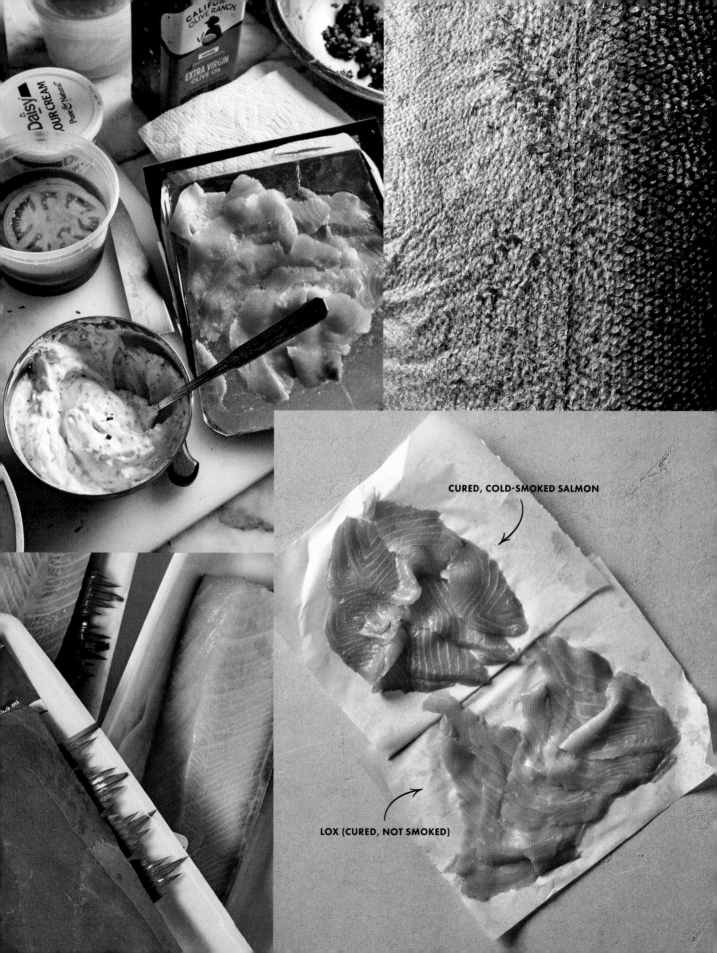

CURED, COLD-SMOKED SALMON

LOX (CURED, NOT SMOKED)

# The No-Cook Guide to Fish and Shellfish

## Smoked Fish

When it comes to smoked fish, the main thing to know is the textural difference between hot- and cold-smoked varieties. Salmon, sturgeon, mackerel, and trout can all be hot smoked, which involves a quick soak in brine followed by high-temperature smoking. The texture of hot-smoked fish is similar to that of fresh cooked fish—tender and easy to flake. The flavor, however, is quite intense compared to fresh fish. You can buy it vacuum sealed in the refrigerator section of grocery stores. Cold-smoked fish is first cured, then smoked for longer (than hot-smoked products) at a lower temperature. The finished texture is silky soft but too firm to flake, so it must be thinly sliced to be served. For the visual difference between smoked salmon and lox see page 60.

Salmon, sea-trout, and sturgeon are often cold smoked, while lox is a bit of an outlier in this category. It is not smoked but cured for a longer period than cold-smoked fish, usually over the course of several days.

1. Hot-smoked peppered salmon
2. Cold-smoked salmon trout
3. Cold-smoked mackerel
4. Hot-smoked rainbow trout
5. Cold-smoked halibut

It's important to seek out quality brands and to be especially mindful of how the fish is caught. Look for labels indicating that the fish is line-caught. Responsible brands include Scout, Ortiz, Matiz, Minnow, Nuri, Arroyabe, and Tonnino.

## Fresh Fish and Shellfish

To serve fish raw, make sure the fish is sushi grade, so go to a reliable (not necessarily a supermarket) fresh fish counter or a Japanese or Korean grocery store. The latter are very reasonably priced, their turnover is quick, and they sell just the right size with little waste, if any.

## Tinned Fish

In all supermarkets and specialist food stores, there is a fantastic variety of excellent tinned fish. Many are also available in sealed jars, but they are still referred to as tinned! I stock a selection of tinned mackerel fillets, tuna belly in olive oil, and sardines in a spicy tomato sauce. Oil-packed anchovies are one of my go-to snacks straight out of the refrigerator. Bonus tinned fish varieties include squid in black ink, octopus, smoked mussels, and oysters. The texture of smoked tinned fish tends to be drier than nonsmoked tinned fish.

# Tuna and Tomato Salad

When heirloom tomatoes are in season there's no better base to pair with tuna. I add olives and capers for salt, dandelion, arugula, escarole, endive, or even radicchio for a robust and peppery kick, and to finish, a splash of sherry or malt vinegar. Every mouthful is a perfect flavor bomb.

**SERVES 1**

1 large heirloom tomato, sliced

Extra-virgin olive oil

Sherry or malt vinegar

Sea salt flakes and black pepper

8 pitted kalamata olives, halved

1 large handful coarsely chopped bitter-leaf salad, such as dandelion, then finely chopped

1 Tbsp. capers in brine, drained

1 tin (4oz/ 115g) wild-caught tuna in olive oil, drained

For heat: add 1 tsp. Calabrian chiles in oil (optional)

Something crunchy: lightly crushed sesame or za'atar crackers or furikake (optional)

Scatter the tomatoes on the base of the serving plate, then splash with olive oil and vinegar. Season with salt and pepper. Top with the olives.

In a small mixing bowl, add the chopped salad leaves, capers, and a splash of olive oil and vinegar, and toss well to mix. Pile onto the tomatoes.

Place the tuna directly on top, splash with olive oil and vinegar again, and a sprinkle of sea salt and black pepper. Add the Calabrian chiles for some heat, plus something crunchy, if liked.

# Sardine with Soy-Fermented Egg and Vegetable Bowl

As well as vinegar-pickled vegetables, I'm also a big fan of soy-fermented vegetables, which are available in specialist grocery shops and health food stores. They can be found in vacuum pouches or glass jars in the refrigerator section. Varieties include daikon, carrot, lotus root, burdock root, and cucumbers, all flavored with chiles and ginger. If I'm in a hurry, but I want to make my own Soy-Fermented Eggs (page 20) I use the leftover liquid from these vegetables instead. It's so good.

**SERVES 1**

½ pouch (9oz/250g) quinoa, microwaved for 60 seconds

Splash of extra-virgin olive oil or toasted sesame oil

Sea salt flakes

½ fennel bulb, thinly sliced

3 to 4 slices quick-pickled Watermelon Radishes (page 21)

1 Soy-Fermented Egg, halved (page 20)

2 to 3 heaping Tbsp. ready-made soy-fermented vegetables and/or red kimchi

1 large pinch of microgreens, like radishes, cilantro, or broccoli

1 tin (4oz/115g) sardine or mackerel in extra-virgin olive oil

½ serrano chile, shaved on a mandoline, or 1 heaping Tbsp. pickled jalapeños

Something crunchy: toasted sesame seeds, toasted sunflower seeds, or furikake

Season the quinoa with a little oil and salt, then fluff with a fork. Add to a serving bowl.

Randomly arrange all the salad components over the quinoa, drizzle over a little more oil, and scatter with something crunchy. Serve.

**QUICK SWAP**
Look out for beet-pickled eggs. They are available in many grocery stores, close to the pickled vegetables in the chilled section. They are pink on the outside.

# Tinned Fish Plates

It's become quite a fashionable go-to for restaurants around the world to serve fish directly out of its tin. It's placed on a board with chips or good sourdough bread and other fixings.

### Sardine Platter

Sardines in oil dressed with chopped parsley

Sliced red onions soaked in ice-cold water

Oat or multigrain crackers

Salt and vinegar chips

Store-bought pickled green beans or okra

Chilled light white wine

## Mackerel Plate

Mackerel in extra-virgin olive oil from a jar

Quick-pickled vegetables (page 21) or ready-made giardiniera

Yellow cherry tomatoes on the vine

Schmear of cultured butter sprinkled with sea salt flakes and ground black pepper

Handful of Potato Stix or Pik-Nik

Sesame sourdough baguette

Chilled red wine

## Tuna Plate

Tuna belly in extra-virgin
olive oil, dressed
with chopped chives

Handful of baby arugula
dressed with olive oil and
lemon juice, sprinkle of salt

Fire-roasted red and
yellow peppers,
drained and sliced

Black kalamata olives

Pita chips

Slices of lemon

Salsa Verde (page 24)

Chilled Riesling

## Deluxe Board

Anchovies in oil skewered with Calabrian chile-stuffed green olives

1 tin stuffed squid in ink

1 tin smoked spicy mussels

1 tin smoked razor clams

Sourdough bread

Slab of cultured butter sprinkled with sea salt flakes and marigold petals

Thin slices fresh cucumber and fennel

Caper berries

Few leaves of radicchio

Lemon wedges

Vermouth on ice with orange slices

# Watermelon, Tomato, and Shrimp Salad

The secret flavor-impact ingredient here is fish sauce. It gives a characteristic salty taste to the cooling sweet watermelon. If you find the fish sauce too strong, a good alternative super-impact ingredient is pomegranate molasses, which has a sweet-sharp citrus taste.

**SERVES 4**

13 oz/380g watermelon flesh (a small wedge of melon)

2 heirloom tomatoes

1 lb/450g (26 to 30) cooked shelled large shrimp, thawed if frozen

1 small red onion, thinly sliced and soaked in ice-cold water for 10 minutes, drained

2 Tbsp. extra-virgin olive oil

2 tsp. toasted sesame oil

2 Tbsp. fish sauce or pomegranate molasses

Juice of 2 limes (optional)

Sea salt flakes (optional)

1 handful cilantro leaves

4 radishes, thinly sliced, soaked in ice-cold water, and drained

1 serrano chile, thinly sliced (optional)

4 heaping Tbsp. crispy onions

Crackers, for serving

Cut the watermelon and tomatoes into 1-inch/2.5cm large random chunks. Place in a large shallow dish and add the shrimp and onion.

In a separate bowl, mix the olive and sesame oils and fish sauce or pomegranate molasses together. If using the fish sauce, add the lime juice too. Add to the watermelon salad and toss gently. Taste, adding salt if needed. Let stand for 10 minutes for the flavors to develop.

Divide between individual bowls. To one side of each bowl, randomly place cilantro leaves, radishes, and chile (if using), then scatter with crispy onions. Serve with crackers.

# Mexican Shrimp Cocktail

I love all types of shrimp cocktail, from the British version with a Marie-rose sauce (mayo and ketchup) sitting on crisp shredded lettuce, the American version with a spicy horseradish and tomato sauce to dip the shrimp into, and, my favorite, this Mexican "soupy"-style cocktail, which reminds me of a gazpacho with the finishing touch of Old Bay Seasoning.

**SERVES 4**

1 lb/450g (26 to 30) cooked shelled large shrimp, thawed if frozen

½ cup/120ml V-8 tomato juice, or 1 tomato processed in a blender then strained

4 Tbsp. ketchup

Juice of 3 limes

1 jalapeño, thinly sliced

2 large green celery stalks, thinly sliced

2 heaping handfuls diced cucumbers

1 small handful diced red onions

2 to 3 heaping Tbsp. coarsely chopped cilantro

Old Bay Seasoning, plus extra for serving

1 tsp. Mexican hot sauce or Tabasco

1 medium ripe avocado, diced

½ cup/120ml bottled clam juice

Lime wedges, salty crackers, or lime tortilla chips, for serving

Set aside four to eight shrimp, then chop the remaining shrimp into five pieces each.

In a large bowl, mix the tomato juice with the ketchup and limes (starting with two initially). Add the jalapeño, celery, cucumbers, onions, and cilantro. Add the chopped and whole shrimp. Taste and season with Old Bay Seasoning and hot sauce. Let chill for at least 15 minutes.

To serve, add the avocado and enough clam juice to make the consistency quite soupy.

Remove the whole shrimp and set aside. Divide the remaining mixture between four small bowls and garnish each with the whole shrimp. Serve with lime wedges, salty crackers, or tortilla chips, plus extra Old Bay Seasoning.

# Lobster, Shrimp, and Crab Brioche Rolls

Lobster and crabmeat are available fresh, tinned, or frozen from most grocery stores and fish counters. I prefer to use the variety sold fresh at the fish counters near the smoked salmon area. The shellfish should be sweet-tasting with some obvious lumps of pink meat. Use Old Bay seasoning as the "salt" to season the shellfish rolls.

**SERVES 4**

¾ cup/ 175ml crème fraîche

Grated rind of 1 lemon and juice from ½

1 Tbsp. each of chopped tarragon, chives, dill, and flat-leaf parsley

Old bay seasoning or celery salt

1 lb/ 450g cooked, shelled shellfish meat such as lobster, shrimp, or crabmeat

4 large or 12 mini brioche buns, or brioche dinner rolls

1 handful watercress, arugula leaves, or cilantro microgreens

Half sour pickles, sliced, or pickled jalapeños, plus extra for serving

Chips, for serving

In a bowl, mix the crème fraîche with the lemon rind and juice. Stir in the herbs, then taste, and season with a pinch of Old Bay Seasoning. If using one type of shellfish meat, add to the dressing, if not, divide into however many types of shellfish you are using.

Carefully fold each shellfish into the portioned-out dressing. You want to keep the meat in large pieces.

Split the brioche buns at the top. Place a small sprig or two of watercress or arugula into each bun, then top with the dressed shellfish. Add a slice of half sour cucumber or pickled jalapeño. Sprinkle with a little more Old Bay Seasoning and serve with chips and extra pickles.

# Lox Grain Bowl

What's the difference between lox and smoked salmon? Lox is cured and not smoked, while smoked salmon is cured and always smoked—hence a slightly saltier, smoky flavor.

**SERVES 2**

1 large green tomato

4 Tbsp. sherry wine vinegar

4 Tbsp. extra-virgin olive oil, plus an extra splash

1 tsp. brown sugar

Sea salt flakes and black pepper

1 pouch (9oz/250g) mixed grains, heated in the microwave for 90 seconds

4 oz/115g farmer's cheese or cream cheese

2 heaping Tbsp. crème fraîche or sour cream

3 Tbsp. mixed chopped chives and dill

3 heaping handfuls baby arugula, washed and dried

Ruffles of lox or smoked salmon 8 slices depending on size)

1 large heirloom tomato, coarsely chopped

1 half sour pickle, sliced

Thinly sliced red onions, soaked in ice-cold water for 10 minutes, then drained

2 heaping Tbsp capers in brine, drained

1 to 2 lemon wedges

Something crunchy, such as bagel or pita chips, for serving

Thickly slice the green tomato, then place in a bowl with the vinegar, 4 Tbsp. olive oil, sugar, salt, and pepper. Let stand for 10 minutes while preparing everything else.

Place the grains in a bowl and season with salt and pepper and a splash of oil. Toss with a fork to separate the grains. Taste and adjust the seasoning, if needed.

For the whipped cheese, whisk the farmer's cheese or cream cheese with the crème fraîche until light and fluffy. Fold in the chives and dill. Set aside.

Drain the green tomatoes, setting the liquid aside too.

Dress the arugula with a little of the green tomato dressing.

To assemble, divide the herbed cheese and spread on one side of two serving bowls. Add a pile of grains, followed by the arugula, ruffles of lox or smoked salmon, green tomatoes, red tomato, pickle, and onion rings in the center. Finally, sprinkle with capers, add a wedge or two of lemon, and serve with bagel chips, if liked. Add the green tomato dressing on the side.

**QUICK SWAP**
Of course, you can buy a container of your favorite whipped cream cheese and herb combo and use that instead of making your own.

# Sesame Tuna Tartare

This is one of my go-to dishes in a restaurant either as an appetizer or main course. Salmon can be easily used in place of the tuna.

**SERVES 2**

2 -inch/5cm piece fresh ginger, peeled

Juice of 1 lime

1 Tbsp. toasted sesame oil

2 tsp. toasted sesame seeds

1 serrano chile, finely diced to give 2 tsp. (optional)

12 oz/350g sushi-grade tuna fillet, diced

Sea salt flakes and black pepper

1 large ripe avocado, quartered, pitted, and peeled

Splash of extra-virgin olive oil

1 to 2 tsp. furikake, crispy garlic furikake, or togarashi, plus extra for serving

Tortilla chips, for serving

Grate the fresh ginger on a microplane into a bowl. Put the pulp into a small strainer and press with the back of a small spoon to make ginger juice (you'll make about 2 tsp.). Add half the lime juice to the ginger juice, plus the sesame oil, sesame seeds, and chile (if using). Add the tuna to the ginger dressing and mix well. Taste and adjust the seasoning, if needed.

Dice the avocado into small to medium cubes and place in a bowl. Add the remaining lime juice, salt and pepper, and a little olive oil. Add half of the furikake and mix well. Taste and adjust the seasoning if needed.

Place a 4-inch/10cm cookie cutter in the center of a serving plate. Place half the avocado mixture in the cookie cutter and press gently with the back of a metal spoon to level the surface. Spoon half of the tuna mixture over the avocado, again spreading to the edge of the cookie cutter. Lift the cookie cutter to remove, and repeat on a second plate with the remaining ingredients. Chill until required.

Just before serving, sprinkle with furikake and serve with tortilla chips.

# Poke Bowl

It's very hard to give just one recipe for poke, as you can make endless versions. The fixings are whatever you feel like from nori sheets, bonito flakes, pickled ginger, crunchy salad vegetables, such as cucumber, radishes, edamame, some fruit like mango, papaya, or pineapple, crispy onions, and sesame seeds. You can also replace the rice with salad leaves.

**SERVES 2**

**Base**
- 1 pouch (9oz/250g) white sushi rice, heated in the microwave for 90 seconds
- 1 Tbsp. unseasoned rice vinegar
- 1 tsp. mirin
- 1 pinch of sea salt flakes

**Fish:**
- 12 oz/350g sushi-grade salmon, tuna, or yellowtail
- 1 to 2 tsp. coconut aminos, tamari, or ponzu sauce

**Fixings**
- 1 handful shredded red cabbage seasoned with lemon juice and salt
- 1 handful thinly sliced cucumbers or radishes
- 1 handful edamame, thawed in cold water if frozen
- 2 heaping Tbsp. cubed mango
- Sushi pickled ginger
- Sriracha mayo
- Salmon or flyfish roe
- Crispy onions or furikake
- Nori sheets, for serving

Place the rice in a bowl and season with the vinegar and mirin. Stir with a fork, keeping the grains separate. Taste and season with salt, if needed.

Cut the fish into cubes, about ½-inch/1cm thick. Place in a bowl and season with the coconut aminos, tamari, or ponzu sauce, starting with 1 tsp. initially. Taste, adding more sauce and a little salt, if needed. Chill in the refrigerator until required.

Organize all your fixings, then start to assemble. Divide the rice between two serving bowls (you don't want too much). Top with piles of red cabbage, cucumber slices, edamame, the seasoned fish, mango, and pickled ginger. Drizzle with the Sriracha mayo, add a pile of fish roe in in the center, scatter over the crispy onions or furikake, and place a couple of sheets of nori on the side of the bowl to serve.

**QUICK SWAP**
Look for the freshest raw fish, a sushi-grade fish is important. If you get scared, you can use cooked shrimp (fresh, or thawed if frozen).

# Simple Ceviche

It's easy and quick to make ceviche. I've tasted quite a few and one of my favorites is the Peruvian one that uses hot yellow peppers—Aji Amarillo. You can buy a sauce made from this pepper online, called Yellow Hot Pepper Ceviche. I like to serve ceviche over white rice (not very Peruvian, but I prefer it to the traditional mashed potato). Use sushi-grade fish available from specialist grocery stores or good fish counters. I trust their level of freshness and it gives me a peace of mind when serving "raw" cured fish.

**SERVES 4 AS AN APPETIZER OR 2 AS A MAIN COURSE**

12 oz/350g firm sushi-grade white fish such as snapper, striped bass, or red snapper

1 small handful thinly sliced shallot or red onion

1 tsp. finely chopped Fresno chile

1 to 2 heaping Tbsp. chopped cilantro, plus extra for sprinkling

½ cup/120ml yellow hot pepper ceviche sauce

Juice of 1 lemon and 1 lime, mixed

Extra-virgin olive oil

Lime wedges, fresh sliced radishes, tortilla or plantain chips, salty chips, or crackers, for serving

Cut the fish into ½-inch/1cm dice. Place in an ice-cold bowl and mix in the shallots, chile, and cilantro. Mix the yellow hot pepper sauce with the citrus, add to the fish, and mix well. Add 1 to 2 Tbsp. ice-cold water depending on the consistency you'd like the sauce to be. Chill for 15 minutes.

Divide the ceviche between two shallow serving bowls. Drizzle over a little olive oil and a squeeze of lime juice. Sprinkle with a little more cilantro. Serve with radishes and chips.

# Fish Crudo

Crudo uses the freshest of sushi-grade fish, which is quickly cured with lemon juice and served at once, while ceviche has triple the amount of acid and cures for longer, changing the texture of the fish. Serve over salad leaves.

**ALL RECIPES SERVE 2 TO 4**

## Mackerel with Cherry Tomatoes

Thinly slice 8oz/225g sushi-grade mackerel or snapper fillet and arrange on a serving plate.  Drizzle with the juice of 1 lemon. Smash a handful of mini yellow cherry tomatoes and drizzle with **extra-virgin olive oil**. Spoon over the fish. Season with **sea salt flakes and black pepper**. Finish with **cilantro or bulls blood microgreens**, if available. Serve.

## Scallops with Grapefruit

Thinly slice **4 sushi-grade scallops** into 3 to 4 disks. Arrange on a serving plate and squeeze ½ **grapefruit** over the top. Remove the **flesh from the other grapefruit half** and place over the scallops. Add **2 Tbsp. finely diced avocado**, then drizzle with **extra-virgin olive oil**, and season with **sea salt flakes** and **salsa seca (Xilli, see page 17)**. Serve.

## Hamachi with Coconut Milk and Lime

Thinly slice **8oz/225g hamachi** (yellowtail), sprinkling with the **juice of 1 lime**. Drizzle with **2 tsp. toasted sesame oil** and **1 to 2 Tbsp. coconut milk**, then sprinkle with **toasted sesame seeds** and **sea salt flakes**. If you have any **shiso or cilantro microgreens**, sprinkle those over the top to finish. Serve.

## Tuna Crudo with Salsa Verde

Thinly slice 8oz/225g sushi-grade tuna and arrange on a serving plate. Drizzle with the juice of 1 lemon and spoon over 2 Tbsp. Salsa Verde (page 24). Add shaved fresh serrano chile for a pepper-hot impact. Serve.

# Smoked Fish Board for a Crowd

This is quite the spread when entertaining or having a few people over. Serve two or three different smoked fish—I love a big gold cold-smoked mackerel, cold-smoked salmon or trout as well as flaked hot-smoked salmon or trout fillets, and a tin of smoked mussels.

**SERVES 6**

### Salad

- 2 to 3 handfuls mixed torn bite-size pieces escarole
- 1 little gem lettuce, separated
- Extra-virgin olive oil
- Lemon juice
- Sea salt flakes and black pepper

### Smoked Fish

- 1 whole cold-smoked mackerel, some of the top skin removed
- 2 (4oz/110g) fillets hot-smoked peppered salmon or trout, skin discarded and flaked
- Quarter side of boned smoked trout fillet, cut into thin slices
- 1 to 2 tins (4oz/110g) smoked mussels in oil

### Fixings

- 2 handfuls sugar snap peas
- 1 handful each sliced dill pickles, caper berries, sprouted lentils or mung beans, thinly sliced red onions, cucumbers, and halved yellow cherry tomatoes
- Lemon wedges
- 1 quantity Avocado and Yogurt Dressing (page 24) or plain Greek yogurt
- Sliced sourdough and variety of crackers, for serving

Place the salad ingredients in a large bowl and toss with a couple of drizzles of olive oil and lemon juice. Season with salt and pepper. Randomly pile the salad greens over a serving board.

Add the fish in three definite places, keeping well apart.

Now start to add piles of the other fresh ingredients and pickles around the fish. Make room for the smoked mussels. Add lemon wedges and a couple of bowls of the dressing to be used as spreads or just a pot of Greek yogurt. Serve the sourdough bread and crackers on the side.

**SERVING TIP**
This alternative way of serving smoked salmon or trout may baffle a few people. Simply eat like ruffles of smoked salmon, but make sure to remove the skin. You can also use ruffles of smoked salmon or lox.

# Smoked Trout, Sugar Snap, and Quinoa Pilaf

I have not given a recipe for tzatziki as there are so many to choose from in every supermarket and small corner store. If you are stuck, simply grate a small Persian cucumber on the large holes of a box grater, squeeze the water out, and mix in 4 Tbsp. thick Greek-style yogurt. Season to taste.

**SERVES 2**

1 pouch (9oz/250g) quinoa or mixed grains, heated for 90 seconds in the microwave

Extra-virgin olive oil

1 handful sugar snap peas

1 large scallion, cut into 2-inch/5cm long matchsticks

2 radishes, thinly shaved

1 tsp. wholegrain mustard

Juice of ½ lemon

1 large handful pitted green olives, chopped

2 to 4 heaping Tbsp. tzatziki, Greek yogurt, or labneh

2 (4oz/110g) hot-smoked trout fillets

1 handful small mint leaves

1 handful small flat-leaf parsley sprigs

Lemon wedges, for serving

Empty the cooked grains into a large bowl and add a glug of oil. Toss with a fork to separate the grains. Set aside.

Fill a large bowl with cold water and add lots of ice. Add the sugar snaps, scallion, and radishes and let soak for 10 minutes. The scallions should start to curl.

Remove the sugar snaps and slice very thinly on the bias. Add to the grains.

To make the dressing, whisk the mustard, lemon juice, and about 3 Tbsp. extra-virgin olive oil together. Toss into the grain bowl, adding the olives. Drain the scallions and radishes, pat dry, then set a handful aside for garnish. Mix the rest in with the sugar-snap mixture.

To assemble, swirl the tzatziki over the base of two shallow bowls and top with the sugar snap pilaf. Remove and discard the skin from the trout. Flake the fish and mix with the reserved radishes, scallions, and herbs. Pile onto the pilaf. Serve with lemon wedges.

# Taramasalata for Dinner

This is my Greek Cypriot go-to when I just don't know what to have for dinner, but I want something with flavor. A dollop or two of store-bought taramasalata with pita bread, salad, and pistachios is my perfect fix.

### Taramasalata Plate

Place **2 heaping Tbsp. store-bought taramasalata** on a serving plate, add **radishes**, **little gem lettuce**, and sticks of **cucumber** and **celery**. Drizzle with **extra-virgin olive oil**, then sprinkle with **sea salt and pepper**. Serve with **pita chips** or **sesame breadsticks**, plus some **pistachios** and a chilled glass of dry **Oloroso sherry**. Serves 1

Taramasalata is a flavor-packed fish roe spread often served for mezze at a Greek feast.

## Taramasalata Toast

Sometimes, I will make a sourdough taramasalata toast—I brush **a slice of sourdough bread** with **olive oil** and toast over the open flame on my stove. Then I spread **2 heaping Tbsp. store-bought taramasalata** on top and add **shaved radishes, cucumbers, capers,** and a big pinch of **chopped flat-leaf parsley.** To finish, I drizzle with a little **toasted sesame oil.** Serves 1

# Springtime Fattoush with Shrimp

You can use ready-cooked cocktail shrimp from the fish counter or thawed frozen shelled cooked shrimp in this recipe. Alternatively, use hot-smoked salmon—plain or with black peppercorns, with the skin removed, and broken into large flakes. What is Fattoush? See page 176.

**SERVES 4**

1 medium fennel, trimmed and thinly sliced, fronds set aside

1 Persian cucumber, or ½ English cucumber, sliced

½ bunch dandelion greens, cut into 2-inch/5cm pieces

2 small shallots, thinly sliced

2 large handfuls heirloom cherry tomatoes, halved

1½ lb/750g cooked cocktail shrimp

**Dressing**

2 tsp. sumac

½ to 1 tsp. Aleppo pepper

Juice of 1 lemon, plus extra for needed

2 garlic cloves, grated on a microplane

½ cup/120ml extra-virgin olive oil

Sea salt flakes

**To finish**

2 handfuls mixed cilantro microgreens, fresh mint, and flat-leaf parsley

2 handfuls pita chips or light crisp flatbread with za'atar

Place the fennel, cucumber, and dandelion leaves in a large bowl with the shallots, tomatoes, and shrimp and toss to mix.

In a separate bowl, mix the sumac, Aleppo pepper, lemon juice, and garlic together. Start to whisk in the oil until thick. You might not want to add all the oil if it seems thick enough for you. Season to taste with salt.

Add half the dressing to the salad mix and massage the mixture with your hands to coat well with the dressing. Taste and adjust the seasoning with more lemon juice and salt. Let stand at room temperature for 10 minutes for the flavors to infuse.

Add the mixed microgreens and herbs to the salad and toss to mix, adding a little more dressing, if needed. Finally, fold in the chips at the last minute. Serve with extra dressing.

# Smoked Mackerel with Remoulade

Remoulade is a simple crunchy salad of celery root and a creamy mayo-based dressing, which is perfect for smoked fish. You can combine fennel, celery, and celery root, mixing that whole vegetable family together. Surprisingly, carrot is also part of this vegetable family.

**SERVES 4**

1 whole cold-smoked mackerel

**Remoulade**

4 handfuls celery root sticks, about 2 inch/5cm long, ¼ inch/5mm thick, soaked in ice-cold water

2 tsp Dijon mustard

Juice and rind of 1 lemon

2 heaping Tbsp. egg-based mayo

2 Tbsp. crème fraîche

Sea salt flakes and black pepper

**Salad**

2 handfuls baby arugula or 1 large handful large arugula leaves

1 handful watercress sprigs

1 handful mint leaves

Drizzle of extra-virgin olive oil

**Fixings**

Thinly sliced seeded bread

Mixed fresh shaved radishes

Schmear of cultured butter

Well-chilled natural wine of your choice—a chilled red or orange wine is good with smoked fish

To make the remoulade, drain and pat-dry the celery root and place in a mixing bowl.

For the dressing, mix the mustard, lemon rind and juice of ½ the lemon, the mayo, and crème fraîche. Taste and start to season with salt and pepper and extra lemon, if liked. Mix the mayo dressing into the celery root and spoon into a serving bowl.

To assemble, place the fish on a large serving platter, add the bread, radishes, butter, and remoulade. Dress the salad leaves and herbs in a large bowl with a drizzle of olive oil, a squeeze of the remaining lemon half, salt, and pepper. Serve with a well-chilled wine.

**SERVING TIP**
To eat whole cold-smoked mackerel—remove the skin and flake from the bone.

# Cold Cuts

*Sandwiches and Salads*

Whether you are looking at your local deli or the deli-counter at the grocery store, the cold-cut possibilities are almost limitless. Cold cuts, such as smoked and unsmoked hams, thinly sliced peppered beef, pastrami, fresh roasted turkey and chicken are all excellent in salads, sandwiches, and many no-cook recipes.

Next time you are in the local Italian deli or neighborhood grocery store, look up—you'll see that the walls are stocked from floor to ceiling with all kinds of treasures; picture salami and hams hanging from the rafters. And the shelves are stacked deep with all manner of pickled vegetables and olives.

I am very aware of trying to eat in a healthy way, therefore for me the best way to achieve this is to accept that all food is fine in moderation. For cold cuts, it's especially important to choose cured meats and processed sausages wisely; opt for low-sodium and low-nitrate varieties, and even no sulphates. It's all clearly labeled, and you can ask the counter staff for advice, too.

## PREP TIPS

- When buying freshly cut cold cuts, ask the deli person to make sure paper/ or parchment are layered between every few slices; otherwise, the meat sticks together and is impossible to separate once you are home.

- When buying freshly sliced cold cuts, ask the deli person to check with you first on the thickness needed. Thin slices are ideal; avoid wafer-thin as each slice will be filled with holes.

- One of my favorite places to shop for cold cuts is a little extravagant, but it is Eataly. All the precut slices have been done in house, and the turnover is so fast; I feel everything is fresh.

Clockwise from top left: Pastrami; preparation of bresaola carpaccio (page 110); variety of breads (sourdough, sesame baguette, and ciabatta); Mediterranean Pork Sandwich (page 119); variety of olives (marinated mixed Greek olives; spice-brined green olives; oil-cured black olives; pitted Castelvetrano olives).

# The No-Cook Guide to Cold Cuts

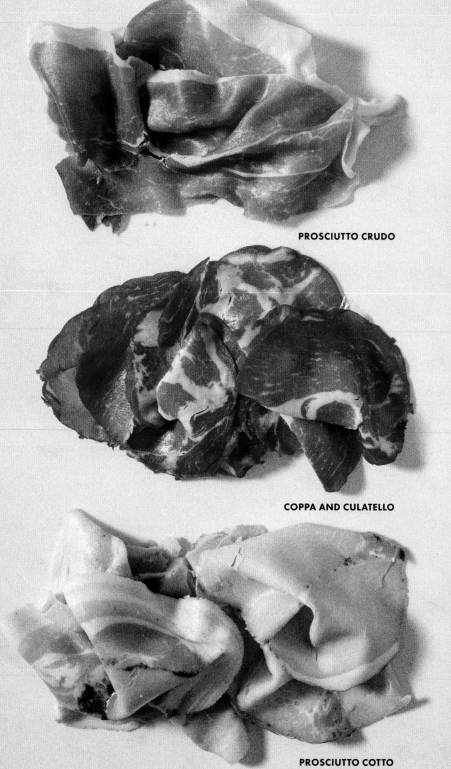

**PROSCIUTTO CRUDO**

**COPPA AND CULATELLO**

**PROSCIUTTO COTTO**

## Prosciutto

Prosciutto is the catch-all name for ham in Italy. It is preserved or cured. Even the ready-sliced pre-packaged prosciutto is not processed; it comes from a joint of shoulder, leg, or butt.

Prosciutto crudo is the name for "raw," cured from the hind leg of the pig or hog. The prosciutto di Parma or San Daniele style (that we hear about) has a light pink, softer texture than other Italian prosciutto crudo like culatello, which comes from the choicest part of the thigh. Coppa crudo comes from the neck fillet. Both these hams have muscle and marbling throughout, giving it a redder appearance. And there are more, all depending on the Italian regions and traditions.

Luckily, many varieties of prosciutto crudo are available overseas, and have become more affordable in recent years, allowing us to enjoy them at home. Yes, there are still the D.O.P. varieties, which are super delicious, for sure, and pricy. Toscana, or prosciutto di Modena hams are a little more reasonably priced. The best way to learn is to take the time and talk to the person at the deli-counter, then sample a piece and see what you prefer. Most grocery store delis are amenable to offering samples.

Prosciutto cotto is cooked ham. Cotto meaning cooked in Italian.

## Mortadella

Mortadella is a sausage, but not a salami. It includes pork, often ground, and is flavored with myrtle and pistachio.

## Pastrami

Pastrami also needs a shout out, as it's so much about its mix of spices—black pepper, coriander, and a citrus tang. Originally made from beef brisket, but lamb, pork, chicken, and turkey can also be treated in the same way. It is brined, partially dried, seasoned with spices and herbs, then smoked and steamed.

## Poultry

Chicken and turkey cold cuts are very popular. Available already sliced from a deli-counter. Sometimes they are not processed; just the actual breast of the bird is cured, flavored, and steamed.

## Salami

Salami is a processed sausage made from pork and beef, chopped in various fine-ish pieces, usually flavored with garlic and spices, notably black pepper. The variety of salami is wide-ranging, especially in grocery stores. The types available include soppressata (pictured, top), Genoa (middle), pepperoni (bottom), Felino, peppered salami, wine salami, and finocchiona.

# Fall Salad with Prosciutto

I like to serve a big seasonal salad with prosciutto straight from the deli packaging. On serving, the intention is to roll the salad in the ham and eat it with any of the other optional extras, such as more Parmesan, toasted almonds or hazelnuts, various marinated olives, and pickles.

**SERVES 4**

1 large bunch Tuscan kale

1 small head escarole

1 quantity vinaigrette, Mustard or Black Garlic (page 23)

1 to 2 ripe Bosc or Asian pears

2 handfuls shaved fancy aged Parmesan cheese, plus an extra piece of cheese for the side

2 handfuls walnut halves, toasted, if liked

20 to 24 slices prosciutto of choice

Optional: Also serve breadsticks, mixture of olives, banana pickles, pickled okra, and other nuts such as roasted hazelnuts or salted Marcona almonds

Remove the stalks from the kale and discard. Tear the kale and escarole into bite-size pieces, wash, and spin dry (or pat dry on a dish towel).

Place the salad leaves in a large serving bowl and rub the leaves with half the vinaigrette, massaging them with your hands. Leave for 10 minutes. The leaves will become tender.

Cut the pears in half and thinly slice on a mandoline, discarding the very central core. Add to the salad leaves, with the shaved Parmesan and walnuts, then add a little more dressing and toss well.

Serve the prosciutto on the side, straight off the paper it was wrapped in. Add the other optional extras if you like, and serve.

**FLAVOR SWAP**
Fall and winter leaves are kale and escarole; for spring, the tender dandelion leaves and Castelfranco salad leaves can be used with persimmons; and for summer, young arugula and radicchio paired with juicy peaches or nectarines.

# Small Italian Plates with Aperitifs

These quick-fix plates use three to five ingredients and take no time to assemble for an aperitif snack.

**ALL RECIPES SERVE 1**

## Panino Plate

Split open a 5-inch / 13cm square of focaccia and drizzle one side with **extra-virgin olive oil**. Season with **sea salt flakes** and pepper and spread with **1 tsp. Calabrian chili paste**. Lay **2 to 4 slices of prosciutto** on top, then **2 slices of provolone**, plus a **handful of arugula**. Sandwich and cut into two. Serve with chilled **Amaro** with **sparkling water**.

## Soppressata Plate

Arrange **3 to 5 spicy slices of soppressata salami** on a plate and lay **2 slices of creamy Taleggio cheese** near them. Add a small pile of **ready-made pickled green beans** and **1 to 2 hot pepperoncini**. Serve with **crispbread** and a chilled red wine such as **Valpolicella** or **Barbera d'Asti.**

## Bresaola Plate

Lay **3 to 4 bresaola slices** all over a serving plate. Thinly slice **1 head of endive** into long shreds and scatter over the meat. Top with torn **figs** or **dark cherry tomatoes**. Drizzle with **extra-virgin olive oil** and season with **freshly ground black pepper**. Serve with **dark sourdough bread** accompanied with an **Americano** —**Campari** with **Vermouth, ice,** and **orange slice**.

## Mortadella Plate

Ruffle 2 to 3 mortadella with pistachio slices on a serving plate. Tear some **buffalo mozzarella** and place near the cold cut. Mix **1 tsp.** Calabrian chili paste with **1 Tbsp.** extra-virgin olive oil and drizzle over. Add **Castelvetrano green olives**, pitted and torn in half, and serve with **crackers** accompanied with a **chilled natural orange wine**.

# Italian Cold Cuts with Marinated Artichokes

When putting together an Italian platter of cold cuts to serve four people try to have at least three different kinds, choosing from prosciutto crudo, prosciutto cotto, mortadella, speck, coppa, and culatello. Marinated artichokes are the perfect accompaniment as the oil is drizzled over the meat to add a rich, nutty, sweet (similar to pistachio), and savory/umami flavor.

**SERVES 4**

1 lb/450g thinly sliced mixed variety of pork charcuterie, selecting the different prosciuttos and mortadella

4 to 6 marinated artichoke hearts with stems in oil

Ready-made pickled vegetables such as okra, green beans, and/or carrots

4 to 6 Belgian endive—red and green (cut into thin spears) or torn radicchio and escarole leaves

1 quantity Salsa Verde (page 24)

Sesame sourdough crusty bread and herb breadsticks, for serving

Ruffle, or arrange however you want, the meats on a platter or individual plates. Add a marinated artichoke on top of each pile with some pickled vegetables. Drizzle over oil from the artichoke jar. Place a pile of endive leaves nearby, add a bowl of Salsa Verde and serve with the bread.

**FRESH TIP**
If you happen to come across tender baby artichokes in season, tear down the leaves to the inner hearts and light leaves (they should not have a hairy choke), and shave into a medium bowl. Cover with extra-virgin olive oil and a couple of chiles. Let stand in the refrigerator for 24 hours, or a few hours at room temperature before using.

# Pastrami Salad Rolls

The best pastrami I ever had was from Paulina in Chicago. The mix of spices, the texture—kind of compressed—was not too different to dry-aged bacon and was just so good.

**SERVES 4**

2 medium carrots, peeled

1 handful snow peas

2 Persian cucumbers

2 large scallions

1 small red onion

2 radishes

2 big handfuls mixed mint, Thai basil, and cilantro

### Dressing

2 Tbsp. fish sauce

1 Tbsp. toasted sesame oil

1 tsp. soy sauce

Juice of 1 lime

### Assemble

8 to 12 slices pastrami

3 heads little gem or 1 head butter lettuce, leaves separated

2 radishes, shaved

2 handfuls mint leaves

2 Tbsp. chopped peanuts

1 quantity Creamy Peanut Butter and Soy Sauce Dressing (page 23) or store-bought peanut dressing

Lime wedges

For the salad, cut all the vegetables into long sticks, about 2 inches/5cm long, and soak in a bowl of ice-cold water for 20 minutes. Drain. Mix the herbs and vegetables together.

For the dressing, mix the fish sauce, sesame oil, and soy sauce with the lime juice. Taste. Toss the dressing and salad ingredients together.

Roll the salad into each piece of pastrami. Arrange on a platter or individual plates with the lettuce, radishes, and mint leaves on the side. Add the dressing and sprinkle with peanuts.

To eat, simply place a pastrami roll in a lettuce cup, add a mint leaf, radish. Serve with the peanut butter dressing and lime wedges.

**FLAVOR SWAP**
You can use different roasted cold cuts, such as peppered beef, chicken or turkey breast, or pork loin from the deli counter.

# Platter of Lentils, Salami, and Oranges

Orange, lentils, and fennel are a classic combination. When serving this salad, I like to arrange all the components separately on a large platter for everyone to have a clear view of the ingredients and so nothing gets lost.

**SERVES 4**

1 head radicchio, torn into large pieces

2 medium fennel bulbs, thinly sliced or shaved

4 radishes, thinly sliced

1 can (15oz/425g) lentils, drained and rinsed

8 oz/225g Genoa or spicy hot salami, cut into sticks

2 blood oranges, peeled with pith removed, cut into slices

1 handful chopped dill

1 handful chopped flat-leaf parsley

Soft ciabatta or focaccia bread, for serving

### Dressing

Juice of 1 to 2 blood oranges

1 tsp. wholegrain mustard

6 Tbsp. extra-virgin olive oil

Sea salt flakes and black pepper

On a large platter, arrange all the ingredients in a haphazard, random manner, starting with the radicchio, then fennel and radishes, adding piles of the lentils, followed by piles of the salami, then the orange slices.

Make the dressing by mixing the orange juice, mustard, and olive oil together. Taste and season with salt and pepper. Drizzle over the salad.

Mix the chopped herbs together and place big pinches all over the platter. Serve with ciabatta or focaccia bread.

**SERVING TIP**
This is one of my favorite salads, and it pairs well with a glass of red wine. I choose natural reds as they are most likely not to contain sulphates. Some of my favorite red wines are from the Piemonte region of Italy. The grapes used are mostly Barbera, Croatina, and Dolcetto.

# Mediterranean Pork Sandwich

This is a mix of Italian and Greek mainstay ingredients. Use either light, fluffy ciabatta bread or herbed focaccia. I love roasted porchetta, the thinly sliced pork loin with a spiral of herbs inside, also known as prosciutto arrosto Toscano, plus rich marinated feta, fire-roasted peppers, and olives—just perfect.

**SERVES 2**

4 Tbsp. extra-virgin olive oil

2 Tbsp. malt or sherry vinegar

1 big pinch of dried or fresh oregano or rosemary

4 thick slices ciabatta bread

1 big handful torn radicchio leaves

2 large yellow or red heirloom tomatoes, cut into ¼ inch/5mm thick slices

6 oz/175g sliced porchetta

1 small red onion, thinly sliced, soaked in ice-cold water for 10 minutes, then drained

1 Persian cucumber, thinly sliced

Sea salt flakes and black pepper

1 cup/115g fire-roasted red and yellow peppers, cut into strips

1 handful pitted kalamata olives, each torn in half

6 large cubes of feta or goat cheese, marinated oil

Something crunchy: Chip Stix

In a small bowl, mix together the oil, vinegar, and herbs. Brush one side of each bread slice with the dressing.

On two slices of bread, dressing-side up, add the radicchio and tomatoes and top with ruffles of porchetta, onion, and cucumber. Drizzle with the dressing and season with salt and pepper. Add the peppers, olives, and marinated cheese.

Sandwich each filling with the bread, dressing-side down. Press down and secure with a toothpick or two, then cut each sandwich in half. Serve with something crunchy and a glass of red wine.

**FLAVOR SWAP**
The porchetta can be subbed with roasted ham or thinly sliced salami—soppressata or finocchiona would be good.

# Mortadella Wedges

I was once offered a steak knife with a classic wedge salad I had ordered in a restaurant, which was a brilliant idea, as it made it so much easier to cut through that mountain of lettuce.

**SERVES 4**

**Caper and White Bean Cream**

- 1 can (15oz/425g) white beans, drained and rinsed
- ½ cup/120ml sour cream
- 4 Tbsp. capers in brine, drained
- 2 Tbsp. brine from capers
- Sea salt flakes and black pepper

**Wedges**

- 1 head iceberg lettuce
- 1 large head radicchio lettuce
- Squeeze of lemon juice
- Drizzle of extra-virgin olive oil
- 2 handfuls finely chopped salted pistachios, toasted sunflower seeds, or crispy onions
- 8 to 12 slices mortadella with pistachio
- 8 oz/225g shaved Parmesan cheese or crumbled creamy blue cheese such as Roquefort or Dolcelatte
- Shaved radishes, for serving

Make the caper and white bean cream by processing all the ingredients in a Vitamix, food processor or stick blender until smooth. Taste and season with salt and pepper, if needed.

Cut each head of lettuce into four wedges, then drizzle each with lemon juice, olive oil, salt, and pepper.

Spread one side of each of the lettuce wedges with the caper and white bean cream, then sprinkle that side with chopped pistachios, sunflower seeds, or crispy onions, or a mixture.

Spread some of the white bean cream on the base of four serving plates and place two lettuce wedges on each. Ruffle three pieces of mortadella on each plate, then scatter over the cheese and radishes. Serve.

**QUICK SWAP**
You can use labneh in place of the caper and white bean cream, and just scatter the capers with the radishes.

# Turkey Tonnato

Traditionally this is made with poached veal, but you can also use veal from the deli counter, although I prefer to use turkey breast instead. I know this dish is normally served as an appetizer, but I like it as my main course as I don't like sharing. Even though it looks bland the flavors are unbeatable. The food stylist in me adds some arugula and yellow cherry tomatoes to finish the plate (and it does complement the dish well), and some green olives and cornichons on the side are perfect too.

**SERVES 2**

**Tonnato Sauce**

- 1 tin (4oz / 115g) tuna in oil, drained
- 3 Tbsp. capers in brine, drained
- 3 anchovies in oil, drained
- 2 Tbsp. sherry vinegar
- 4 to 6 Tbsp. extra-virgin olive oil
- 4 heaping Tbsp. mayonnaise
- Sea salt flakes and black pepper

**Turkey base**

- Thinly sliced turkey breast from the deli—4 slices per person
- 1 large handful arugula
- 1 handful cherry tomatoes (sungolds), halved
- Drizzle of extra-virgin olive oil
- Grissini sticks, crackers, or sourdough bread, for serving

Place all the sauce ingredients in a blender or Vitamix and whizz until super smooth. Taste and adjust with salt, pepper, and maybe a bit more vinegar, if necessary. You will have more sauce than you need, so serve more on the side, or use as a simple dip with radishes on another day.

Transfer the turkey to two large flat serving plates. You can ruffle on the plate slightly. Drizzle with the sauce, then top with the arugula and tomatoes and drizzle with a little olive oil and sprinkle with sea salt flakes. Serve with grissini sticks, crackers, or hunks of sourdough bread.

# Muffuletta

No chapter on cold cuts would be complete without a recipe on the classic American-Italian muffuletta sandwich (it originated in New Orleans). Layers of mixed Italian pickles, sliced cheeses, a mix of cold cuts, and bread. Choose a big slab of soft focaccia or ciabatta, or even a seeded baguette to catch all the juices from the pickles. It's not quite ready in five minutes, but it's well worth the wait for game night or a beach-day picnic.

**SERVES 8**

1 cup/ 115g jarred fire-roasted peppers or piquillo peppers, drained

1 cup/ 110g giardiniera pickles, including the garlic, drained

1 cup/ 125g pitted big green olives in brine, drained

1 handful flat-leaf parsley sprigs

1 Tbsp. capers in brine, drained

1 tsp. dried oregano

1 to 2 heaping Tbsp. Calabrian chili paste

3 Tbsp. red wine vinegar

4 Tbsp. extra-virgin olive oil

1 large whole loaf of bread—ciabatta, focaccia, or seeded baguette

6 oz/ 175g thinly sliced mortadella

8 oz/ 225g thinly sliced soppressata or Genoa salami

6 oz/ 175g thinly sliced prosciutto

2 balls buffalo mozzarella, torn into pieces and drained

8 slices provolone

To make the pickle spread, place the peppers, pickles, and olives in a food processor with the parsley, capers, oregano, chili paste, vinegar, and olive oil and process until quite fine. Taste and season with extra chili paste, if needed.

Cut open the loaf of bread and spread both sides with equal amounts of the pickle spread, taking it right out to the edges.

Start layering the mortadella on the base of the bread, followed by the salami, prosciutto, mozzarella, then the provolone.

Sandwich with the second piece of bread and press down well. Wrap in baking parchment then foil. Press down along the length with a sheet pan, then a cast-iron skillet or cans of tomatoes. Let stand in a cool place for at least 30 minutes or 2 hours. If transporting the sandwich, place in the base of the cooler if you are off to a picnic, and let everything else weigh it down.

Cut into 8 to 12 squares to serve.

Opposite: Making of Muffuletta—prepared pickle spread, piles of prosciutto and mortadella, and loaf of ciabatta bread. This page: Assembled Muffuletta being pressed down with a cast-iron flat-top.

# Salami, White Bean, and Burrata Salad

Cheese, beans, and salami all combine to make this a very easy salad. If liked, a few slices of blood orange or cara cara orange would be a welcome addition. Some wine—a chilled natural orange wine from the winery Rivera Del Notro—is also excellent with the spicy soppressata.

**SERVES 4**

**White Bean Spread**

- 1 can (15oz / 425g) white beans, drained and rinsed
- 2 heaping Tbsp. Greek yogurt
- 1 preserved lemon, halved to remove all pips

  Sea salt flakes and black pepper

**Salad plate**

- 8 oz / 225g burrata, torn into four
- 2 handfuls baby spinach, arugula, or torn radicchio leaves
- 8 whole pickled pepperoncini or whichever pickled chiles you have on hand
- 8 oz / 225g spicy soppressata or salami of your choice, cut into thick sticks or thick slices

  Extra-virgin olive oil

  Squeeze of lemon juice

  Bread or crackers, for serving

Set aside 4 Tbsp. of beans to finish the salad. Place the remaining beans, the yogurt, and preserved lemon in a food processor and whizz until super smooth. Taste and adjust the seasoning with salt and pepper.

To assemble, swirl each plate with some of the bean spread with the back of a metal spoon. Add a piece of burrata to each plate, then a pile of spinach, arugula, or radicchio leaves, pepperoncini, and then the salami. Sprinkle over the reserved beans and drizzle everything with extra-virgin olive oil, a squeeze of lemon juice, and salt, and pepper. Serve with bread or crackers, on the side.

**QUICK SWAP**
Make the White Bean Feta Dip (page 153) or use a ready-made white bean dip instead.

# Chicken and Avocado Wrap

The genius part of using collard greens is that the leaf is almost waterproof so everything stays really crisp. It's also as delicious with a tortilla wrap—your choice!

**SERVES 1**

1 large collard or Swiss chard leaf (or two, depending on size)

½ medium avocado, peeled and pitted

Squeeze of lemon juice

Few drops hot sauce like Cholula

3 slices deli-roasted chicken, turkey, or porchetta, depending on size

Large handful cilantro microgreens

1 handful crumbled feta

1 big pinch of pickled jalapeños

Toasted pumpkin seeds, for sprinkling

Remove the stalks from the leaves and lay the leaves, vein-side up, on top of each other if needed, to give you a square-ish shape, about 12 inches/30cm.

Mash the avocado in the center of the collards, leaving a 1-inch/2.5cm border. Drizzle with lemon juice and hot sauce.

Lay the deli meat on top, followed by the microgreens, feta, jalapeños, and pumpkin seeds.

To roll up the wrap: roll up to halfway, bringing in the unfilled edges to enclose the filling at the sides, and continue to roll. Wrap the whole roll in baking parchment, in much the same way, then cut in the middle to serve.

# Charcuterie on a Stick

Every bite of charcuterie is partnered with sharp (pickles, tomatoes, olives), and/or sweet (preserve, fruit, cheese).

**Mortadella, fresh fig, and chili honey**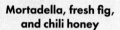

**Fire-roasted pepper, pepperoni, and fontina cheese**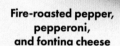

**Prosciutto, peach, and arugula**

**Genoa salami with stuffed green olives and fontina cheese**

Pepperoni, bocconcini, sungold cherry tomato, and basil leaf

Pepperoncini, peppered salami and drizzle of honey

Quartered artichoke hearts in oil, prosciutto, and parsley sprig

Soppressata encasing a schmear of soft goat cheese and quince jelly

Chorizo, Gorgonzola, and cherry tomato

# Grains & Pulses

*Salad Bowls and Dips*

This chapter dives deep into the art of creating meal-in-one "salad" bowls with pulses and grains, and dip platters centered around homemade bean dips or pepped-up store-bought options.

Grains: What a welcome change it is to serve mixed grains like brown, wild, red, purple, and white rice, wheatberries, quinoa, and bulgur instantly, without having to boil them first. These days, precooked grains are sold in pouches in most supermarkets and grocers. The selection of such options is seemingly endless. You can easily reheat the grains in 90 seconds, either in the microwave or by covering them with boiling water in a bowl. Once they are drained, they can be dressed with whatever you feel like.

Pulses: chickpeas, lentils, white beans, black beans, borlotti beans, and more are great sources of plant-based, low-fat protein. You'll find all these in cans, jars, or pouches. Most are unseasoned, but increasingly, there are flavored options, too.

## PREP TIPS

- Standard grain pouches weigh 9oz/250g, about 2 cups worth of grains. If I am cooking for myself, I often heat up half the pouch, and save the other half in the refrigerator for up to three days, and heat when needed.

- Cooking for one: I'll use half a 15oz/425g can of beans, and save the remainder (still in the liquid) in the refrigerator for two to three days.

- When using canned beans and pulses, I like to drain and rinse off the liquid they come in, as I like the cleaner-tasting end result.

Clockwise from top left: Red kimchi; draining canned white beans; microwave-steamed white rice; prepping the Double Chickpea Bean Salad (page 141); array of lettuce—little gem, treviso, and endive.

# White Bean, Pickled Beets, and Radicchio Salad

Add some extra protein to this salad with tinned fish (tuna or mackerel), hot-smoked fish (salmon, mackerel, or trout), rotisserie chicken, blue cheese, goat cheese, or feta.

**SERVES 2**

½ quantity each of pickled red and yellow beets, (page 21), plus some of the pickling juices

Sea salt flakes and black pepper

A few splashes extra-virgin olive oil

1 can or jar (15oz/425g) white beans, drained

2 Tbsp. chopped flat-leaf parsley

1 tsp. wholegrain mustard (optional)

1 small head radicchio, coarsely torn, washed and drained

2 radishes, thinly sliced and soaked in a bowl of ice-cold water for 10 minutes, then drained

4 slices goat cheese

2 Tbsp. something crispy: crispy onions or toasted pumpkin seeds

Mix the pickled red and yellow beets in a bowl and season with pepper and a little olive oil. Set aside.

Place the beans in a bowl and season with some of the beet pickling juices, olive oil, and salt and pepper. Add the parsley. Taste and adjust the seasoning, if needed. Set aside.

Mix 2 Tbsp. pickling juices with a few splashes of olive oil, salt, and pepper, then mix and taste. Add the wholegrain mustard, if liked.

To assemble, dress the radicchio with a little of the dressing and add to the base of two serving bowls. Divide the beans between the bowls, keeping to one side. Add the pickled beets, the radishes, and the sliced goat cheese. Sprinkle with something crispy and serve with any remaining dressing on the side.

# Double Chickpea Salad

The hummus dip gives this salad a much richer and luxurious layer complementing the lighter chickpea, avocado, lettuce, and tomato salad. I like to add a spicy kick to my salads with a chili crisp or a smoky salsa seca.

**SERVES 1**

2 heaping Tbsp. Classic Hummus (page 148 or store-bought)

½ can (15oz/425g) chickpeas, drained

1 big handful shredded lettuce, such as romaine, or arugula, or a mix

1 big handful cherry tomatoes, halved

½ large avocado, flesh removed in teaspoon-style scoops

Extra-virgin olive oil

Pomegranate molasses

Sea salt flakes and black pepper

Something spicy: heat from hot pepper flakes, chili crisp, salsa seca, hot sauce, or sesame chili oil

Something crunchy: pita chips, crispy onions, or toasted sesame seeds

Partially spread the hummus on one side of a serving plate.

In a separate bowl, mix the chickpeas, lettuce, cherry tomatoes, avocado, a drizzle of olive oil, and a drizzle of pomegranate molasses, tossing to mix. Taste and season with salt and pepper, if needed.

Spoon the salad over some of the hummus and the rest of the plate.

Drizzle with something hot and sprinkle with crushed pita chips, crispy onions, or some toasted sesame seeds. Serve.

# Black Beans and Rice with Avocado

This is inspired by the simple side of Mexican black beans and rice. Quinoa, brown rice, or mixed rice can be used instead of the plain white rice. Sometimes, I like to use a store-bought creamy chipotle dressing, which is a combination of smoked hot chipotle peppers and a mayo-style dressing. It's a little smokier than a Sriracha mayo.

**SERVES 2**

1 pouch (9oz/250g) long-grain rice, heated for 90 seconds in the microwave

1 Tbsp. olive oil

1 Tbsp. chopped cilantro, plus 1 small handful cilantro sprigs

Sea salt flakes and black pepper

1 can (15oz/425g) black or pinto beans

1 tsp. chili sesame oil

1 Tbsp. chopped oregano

2 big pieces jarred grilled red or yellow peppers, drained and sliced

2 heaping Tbsp. pickled red onions (page 21)

1 medium avocado, halved, pitted, quartered, and skin removed

1 big handful crumbled cotija, feta, or goat cheese (optional)

1 lime, halved

Tortilla chips

For the dressing: store-bought seeded salsa seca or creamy chipotle dressing

Place the rice in a bowl and fluff up with a fork. Season with olive oil, the chopped cilantro, salt, and pepper. Taste and adjust the seasoning, if needed. Set aside.

Drain the beans into a strainer and rinse under cold water. Shake dry, then place in a bowl and season to taste with the chili sesame oil, oregano, and salt and pepper.

To assemble, place the rice on the base of two shallow serving bowls, gathering a little in one place. Next to that, start to add piles of beans, sliced peppers, drained pickled red onions, and the avocado quarters. Put the cheese in the center (if using). Add the cilantro sprigs, limes, and tortilla chips, then drizzle with your chosen dressing.

**ADD-ONS**
Shaved radishes, cucumber, and fresh jalapeños can also be added.

# Mixed Grains with Kale and Feta

So many people complain, "Not another kale salad," but I love kale because the texture of the leaf holds up well with all types of dressings. Tenderize the robust leaves by massaging with olive oil, lemon juice, and salt, and leave for ten minutes, then continue to build your salad. The kale provides a base for the big flavors of the briny feta and salty olives.

**SERVES 1**

2 heaping handfuls torn Tuscan kale leaves, stalks discarded

1 lemon

Sea salt flakes and black pepper

Extra-virgin olive oil

½ pouch (9oz/250g) mixed grain combo, microwaved for 60 seconds

1 chunk of feta, sliced, or about 1 small handful crumbled

1 handful cherry tomatoes, halved

1 handful pitted kalamata black olives, torn in half

½ medium avocado, peeled and cut into chunks

3 to 4 slices jalapeño (pickled or fresh)

Something crunchy: crushed gluten-free seeded crackers or 1 Tbsp. crunchy corn kernels

Place the torn kale in a large bowl. Grate the lemon rind on top, add 1 Tbsp. extra-virgin olive oil, 3 Tbsp. lemon juice, salt, and pepper and massage together with your hands. Taste for flavor and season a bit more, if needed. Set aside for 10 minutes while preparing everything else.

Place the heated mixed grains in a bowl and flake with a fork. Season with salt and pepper and a drizzle of olive oil.

Pile the mixed grains and kale onto a large serving plate. Add the sliced feta, cherry tomatoes, olives, and avocado. Season with a little more oil and some of the remaining lemon juice. Sprinkle over the jalapeños and crushed seeded crackers. Serve.

# The Dip Platter

What you need to take into consideration when building a platter is how many people you are serving, which dips to have, which crudités, and what's in the pantry. Below, I have some quick suggestions.

## The Building Blocks

### How Many People and Types of Dip

- Single person platter: Serve 3 to 4 Tbsp. of one or two different dips, such as hummus with tzatziki, or eggplant-based dip, an olive-based dip, such as a tapenade.

- Two people: Serve at least two dips—a bean dip and one more, be it yogurt and avocado based, a thick mayo-style, or tapenade; sometimes a thick-dressing can also act as a dip, like a ranch or green goddess.

- Four people: Serve three different dips—dairy-based, some kind of bean-, and avocado-style.

### Crudités

There are no fast rules, but I do give myself a few: I like to stick to color for the vegetables and fruit; this way I think I stay a little sophisticated in my choices. Seasons plays a role for me—especially with my fruit choice.

- Mixing greens with whites and yellows: asparagus, snow peas, sugar snaps, celery, cucumbers, yellow and white/cream carrots; black radish slices; Asian pears, mangoes.

- Pinks and oranges together: dried orange slices, fresh red apples, red endive leaves, red carrots with orange in the middle, dark cherry tomatoes, white peaches with blushed red skins, persimmons.

- All orange and yellow: persimmons (dried or fresh), grapefruit, dried oranges, red endives and radicchio or treviso, red apples, deep red tomatoes, carrots, double-colored carrots (dark red on the outside with orange insides); add some cauliflower and fennel to break up the color a little too.

### Crackers and Chips

- Italian breadsticks and knots: mini taralli rings and tarallini knots, grissini sticks (all thin breadsticks); flat, super thin crackers—pane carasau or the carta di musica (sheets of music); small rectangular croccantini.

- The Portuguese, slightly sweet crackers are good to have on hand.

- Tortilla and pita chips, Middle Eastern sesame or za'atar crisp breads and sesame breadsticks are all good.

- Fresh toasted pita bread and Middle Eastern flatbreads are excellent for bean-based dips.

### Wine Pairings

Bean dips are quite mild in flavor, although they can be pepped up with spice and heat, so for me, light natural wines with a little effervescence (a touch of fizz) are some of my favorites. A well-chilled white or red wine is perfect.

**Opposite: Hummus garnished with crispy chickpeas and microgreens (page 148) and White Bean Feta Dip (page 153).**

# Hummus

Hummus has become one of those go-to foods that can be found in most people's refrigerators. It's a snack for all ages either before dinner or even while preparing dinner. You will never get bored of the variety of flavors available in grocery stores, or even what you can put together at home if you have a can of chickpeas or beans in your pantry.

## Basic Homemade Hummus
**MAKES 1½ CUPS/375ML**

2 Tbsp. tahini paste

Juice of ½ lemon

1 to 2 Tbsp. extra-virgin olive oil

1 can (15oz/425g) chickpeas or white beans, drained, saving about 3 Tbsp. of the liquid

Sea salt flakes and black pepper

Crispy chickpea snacks and sesame or olive oil, for garnishing

In a small bowl, whisk the tahini with 3 Tbsp. water, then add the lemon juice and whisk. Do not add the lemon juice first, as it will make the tahini paste cease. Whisk in the oil.

Place the beans in a Vitamix or food processor with the prepared tahini mix and blend until smooth. Alternatively, use a stick blender. Taste and season with salt and pepper. The level of smoothness is up to you; you can add some of the reserved chickpea liquid and whizz a bit more. I like mine super smooth, which means I might well process for about 5 minutes on and off. Garnish with crunchy salted chickpeas snacks and toasted sesame oil or olive oil.

## Extra Flavor From the Pantry

**Preserved lemon**
Quarter **1 whole preserved lemon** (page 17) and remove the seeds. Add the lemon pieces (flesh and rind), plus **1 Tbsp. toasted sesame oil** to the hummus and process once more until smooth. Hold back on the seasoning until after the preserved lemon is incorporated. Taste and adjust with a tiny pinch of sea salt flakes. Garnish with chopped preserved lemon and **Aleppo pepper**.

**Zhoug**
Add **3 to 4 Tbsp. Zhoug** (page 23 for homemade or use store-bought) to the hummus and process until smooth, then drizzle with an extra 1 to 2 Tbsp. of Zhoug to finish.

**Chili-crisp**
Add **1 Tbsp. Sichuan chili crisp** (page 17) and process until smooth. Garnish with an extra 1 to 2 Tbsp chili crisp to finish.

**Opposite, clockwise from top left: Basic Homemade Hummus, Preserved Lemon, Zhoug, Chili-Crisp.**

# Store-Bought Hummus All Dressed-Up

Transfer the hummus to a shallow bowl, swirl the center with the back of a spoon, then add some simple additions for an instant transformation for appetite appeal and flavor.

**Sliced cucumbers drizzled with sesame chili oil and toasted sesame seeds**

**Fresh sliced serrano chiles, torn nasturtiums, and drizzle of olive oil**

**Store-bought crispy onions and drizzle of olive oil**

Halved cherry
tomatoes dressed
with olive oil,
red wine vinegar, salt,
and flat-leaf parsley

1 to 2 Tbsp.
Mexican salsa seca
(page 17—smoked
chipotle and mixed
seeded oil)

Pinch or two of
spicy microgreens
and drizzle of
toasted sesame oil

# White Bean Dips

A can of white beans and a few fresh ingredients can create a dip with some impressive results both visually and in taste.

Tortilla chips—the best dipping tortilla chips for me are Vista Hermosa. Good crunch, excellent no-break scooping action, and a good flavor.

## White Bean and Avocado Dip

Process **1 can (15oz/425g) white beans**, drained, with **2 big scoops of mayo or Greek yogurt**, **1 medium avocado**, pitted and peeled, **juice of 1 lemon**, and **2 Tbsp. extra-virgin olive oil** until super smooth. Season to taste with **salt**. Fold in **2 Tbsp. Salsa Verde (page 24)**. Transfer to a serving bowl and swirl the top. Drizzle with another **2 Tbsp. Salsa Verde** to serve. Makes 2 cups/500ml

## White Bean Feta Dip

Process **1 can (15oz/425g) white beans**, drained, with **1 Tbsp. chopped shallot**, **2 large handfuls of crumbled feta**, **4 heaping Tbsp. Greek yogurt**, and **2 tsp. toasted sesame oil** until very smooth. Season to taste with a pinch of **salt**. Transfer to a serving bowl and swirl the top with the back of a spoon. Sprinkle with some thinly sliced feta, **1 to 2 pinches za'atar**, and **1 tsp. toasted sesame oil**. Garnish with **marigold petals**. Serve. Makes 1½ cups/375ml

# Pea and Thai Basil Dip

A pea is not a bean, but it is a good source of secondary protein. You can use frozen peas in this dip. To thaw quickly, just soak them in a bowl of cold water for ten minutes, or place them in a colander and run a kettle of hot water through them. Cool before using.

**MAKES 1½ CUPS/375ML**

1 cup/125g thawed frozen garden peas (see intro)

2 handfuls crumbled feta or goat cheese

2 Thai basil or Italian basil sprigs

1 Tbsp. extra-virgin olive oil

Juice of ½ lemon

2 Tbsp. crème fraîche or sour cream

Sea salt flakes and black pepper

Microgreen sprigs of whichever herb used in dip, or petals from edible flowers, and wood sorrel leaves, for garnishing

Crudités: mixed baby carrots, cherry tomatoes, sugar snaps, or young tender asparagus, for serving

Process all the ingredients in a Vitamix, food processor, or using a stick blender to a smooth mixture. Taste and adjust the seasoning, if needed.

Transfer to a board, shallow serving bowl, or several small shallow bowls and finish with microgreen sprigs. Serve with crudités.

# Eastern Mediterranean Pilaf Bowl

The base of this bowl is a mujendra, which is a Cypriot rice and lentil pilaf with lots of fried onions. For this cheat version I combine a pouch of store-bought rice and lentils with pantry crispy onions, extra-virgin olive oil, and lots of fresh herbs.

**SERVES 4**

1 pouch (9oz/250g) rice and lentils, heated in the microwave for 90 seconds

4 Tbsp. extra-virgin olive oil

2 Tbsp. chopped chives or flat-leaf parsley

3 Tbsp. chopped dill

4 Tbsp. crispy onions

Sea salt flakes and black pepper

1 cup/110g ready-made giardiniera mixed pickles (mainly cauliflower and carrot), plus a little of the pickling liquid

1 Tbsp. pomegranate molasses

3 big handfuls mixed baby spinach and torn Tuscan kale

1 Persian cucumber, coarsely chopped

1 heirloom tomato, coarsely chopped

1 small red onion, shaved and soaked in ice-cold water for 10 minutes, then drained

Aleppo pepper (optional)

9 oz/250g halloumi, shredded

8 stuffed vine leaves, canned, jarred, or from the deli counter

Something crunchy: crispy onions or pita chips, for sprinkling

Place the grains in a large bowl and fluff up with a fork, mixing in a splash of olive oil and the herbs. Add the crispy onions and mix once more, stirring gently to keep the grains and crispy onions loose and to avoid crushing them. Taste, adding salt if needed.

Take a little juice from the pickles (2 Tbsp.) and mix with the pomegranate molasses and the remaining olive oil. Season with salt and pepper. Use 3 Tbsp. of the dressing to mix into the spinach and kale mix.

Mix the cucumber, tomato, and onion. Season with salt, Aleppo pepper (if using), and the remaining dressing and mix well. Taste.

To assemble, divide the greens between four serving bowls. To one side of each bowl divide the rice and lentil pilaf, followed by the halloumi, then the cucumber and tomato salad, the pickles, and finally, the stuffed vine leaves. Sprinkle over the crispy onions and Aleppo pepper (if using). Serve with any extra dressing.

**ADD-ONS**
Hummus (page 148), white bean dip, or tzatziki (cucumber and yogurt) are a perfect addition.

# Korean-Style Tofu Grain Bowl

Purple rice, kimchi, tofu, soy-fermented eggs, and shredded scallions are a nod to Korean flavors. All of the ingredients are now available in most grocery stores, and if you go to an H-mart (Korean supermarket) you can even find already shredded scallions and soy-fermented eggs. To make it vegan you can sub the eggs for avocado.

**SERVES 2**

8 oz/225g silken or soft tofu

1 cup/75g red kimchi with juice

1 pouch (9oz/250g) purple rice or mix of quinoa and purple rice (whatever you like and have on hand), heated in the microwave for 90 seconds

1 Tbsp. toasted sesame oil

1 large handful coarsely shredded carrots

1 large handful shredded zucchini

1 handful snow peas, shredded or thinly sliced on the diagonal

3 to 4 Tbsp. sesame dressing of your choice (page 24)

3 heaping handfuls chopped napa cabbage alone or mixed with chopped baby bok choy and kale

2 Soy-Fermented Eggs (page 20)

1 large scallion, thinly sliced into strips, soaked in ice-cold water for 10 minutes, then drained

Something crunchy: toasted sesame seeds

1 lime, halved

Drain the tofu, cut into 1-inch/2.5cm cubes, and place in a shallow bowl. Chop the kimchi and place over the tofu with the kimchi juice. Let stand for 10 minutes.

Place the rice in another bowl and drizzle over the sesame oil. Toss to mix with a fork.

Have all the other elements prepared. Use a little of the sesame dressing to dress the salad leaves.

To assemble, place the dressed salad leaves on the base of two serving bowls. Divide the rice between the bowls, placing in one area, followed by the marinated tofu and kimchi. Continue to add the carrots, zucchini, and snow peas. Cut the eggs in half and add to the bowls. Drizzle with the remaining dressing. Top with the scallions and sprinkle with sesame seeds. Serve with lime halves.

**ADD-ONS**
Spicy chili garlic crisp, or toasted chopped peanuts.

# Corn, Mango, and Tomato Salsa with 7-grains and Salmon

This is definitely a summer recipe when corn is at its best, very tender, and bursting with sweet "milk" so it doesn't need to be blanched or cooked. Mix with heirloom tomatoes, mango, and cilantro. My good friend, Beatriz da Costa, kindly gave me the salsa recipe as I've helped her make it many times to be served with beans, lentils or rice, and fish.

**SERVES 2**

## Salsa

- 1 ear of corn
- 1 large heirloom tomato or 2 handfuls cherry tomatoes
- 1 small champagne mango (for me, the best flavored), peeled
- 1 large basil sprig, torn
- 2 Tbsp. chopped chives or 2 to 3 Tbsp. chopped red onions
- 1 splash of sherry vinegar
- Drizzle of extra-virgin olive oil
- Sea salt flakes and black pepper

## Salad

- 3 large handfuls torn dandelion leaves, radicchio, or endive, washed and dried
- 1 pouch (9oz/250g) 7-grains, microwaved for 90 seconds
- 8 oz/225g hot-smoked salmon or mackerel, flaked into large pieces, skin discarded
- Hot sauce of your choice, such as sesame chili oil, Cholula, or garlic chili oil
- Something crunchy: 1 to 2 Tbsp. sprouted mung beans or crushed gluten-free mixed seed crackers

Husk the corn and cut the corn from the ear into a large bowl, holding the ear over the bowl as you do it to catch any of the sweet juice. Coarsely chop the tomatoes and mango, keeping them quite large. Add to the corn with the basil and chives or onions, then dress with the sherry vinegar and olive oil. Season with salt and pepper. Let stand for 5 minutes, as you want the juice to develop.

Drain the juices created in the salsa, and save it, as you are going to use it as your dressing.

Place the torn salad leaves in a clean bowl and dress with some of the reserved corn dressing.

Flake the mixed grains with a fork, dressing with a splash of olive oil and salt to taste.

To assemble, divide the salad leaves between two serving bowls and add the grains, corn salsa, and flaked fish. Add the hot sauce of your choice, then sprinkle over something crunchy. Serve.

**KEEP OPTIONS OPEN**
The corn salsa is also good served with shrimp or tinned tuna. Now I think about it, it's also perfect with shredded rotisserie chicken, white beans, or chickpeas.

# Cheese

*Plates and Platters to Share*

This chapter considers cheese as the main attraction, rather than just a supporting player to serve at the beginning or end of a meal. Cheese is for everyone, not just the go-to option for vegetarians and snacks.

Cheese provides a springboard for robust peppery salads using radicchio, arugula, and dandelion leaves; sweet, fresh melons and summer stone fruit; and tart and sweet tomatoes of all varieties. They are great partners for salami and sausages of all kind—spicy hot or fragrant fennel for instance; as well as cured and smoked meats and fish. The cheeses are incorporated into salads and grain bowls, as well as presented as a cheese board and platters to be served as a meal.

**PREP TIPS**

- To thinly slice the cheese, chill it first, then cut with a very sharp knife, mandoline, or straight vegetable peeler. Once cut, allow to come to room temperature before serving.

- For these no-cook recipes, avoid using ready-shredded cheese in pouches, as they maybe coated with "something" to keep all the shreds separate in the bags.

- When grating cheese, I like to use the type of microplane with about ¼-inch/5mm straight lines, not little holes, or squares. This allows the cheese to shred into long and airy strips with a melt-in-the-mouth texture.

Clockwise from top left: Membrillo, also known as quince paste, is perfect with all cheese; creamy Vacherin Mont D'or; macerated tomatoes (page 171); mixture of microgreens; persimmons, and mini clementines.

# The No-Cook Guide to Cheese

### White Cheese Club

This is not a real group of cheeses, but one I have made up. The most versatile cheeses to incorporate into simple meals fall into the "white cheese club." These include creamy aged or fresh goat cheese, salty, crumbly feta cheese (no longer reserved for Greek dishes), and fresh ricotta, which provides a base for sharp, sweet, and smoked flavors. Halloumi and ricotta salata have also made their way onto the dinner plate. Their definite salty, sharp flavor provides a contrast to salad, meat, and grain recipes. Finally, not forgetting the fresh mozzarella—buffalo or cow's milk—or the extra luxurious burrata. And I haven't even mentioned the fresh Robiola that is the creamiest of cheeses to spread on a cracker; it's sweet and tangy at the same time.

### Semi-Hard

Semi-hard cheeses such as Comte, Gruyère, fontina, provolone, and cheddar, plus many more, add a satisfying richness to recipes, whether served in slices, pieces, or grated. Yes, their best element is how brilliantly they melt when cooking, but in this book it's about their unctuous contribution to every bite.

## Double and Triple Cream Cheese

La Tur, Brillat Savarin, Saint André, Triple-crème Bries, and Robiola, add a creamy, melting texture with enough flavor to complement additions like nuts, fruits, and spices.

## Blue Cheese

The blue cheese club—Roquefort, Gorgonzola, Cashel blue, and Point Reyes all make good single cheese plates or boards, as well as adding a creamy element to salad and grain bowls.

## Hard

Parmesan and Pecorino Romano will always have a place as mainstays in the refrigerator. These grating cheeses are used endlessly in main courses, salads, and dressings. I like to have them by themselves on a simple plate with seasonal fruit such as persimmons, apples, pears (conventional and Asian), raisins, nuts, and as well as some seeded crackers.

Gorgonzola Dolce, Cashel blue, Roquefort

# Peach, Halloumi, and Purslane Salad

This is a very summery salad making the most of juicy, ripe peaches when they are available. The purslane is a mild-tasting summer leaf, but you can add arugula for a more peppery leaf, or a bitter green, such as radicchio or dandelion to contrast with the rich, sweet peaches. The halloumi is essential to add that salty contrast, so don't add salt until the whole salad is tossed and tasted.

**SERVES 2**

**Dressing**

- 2 Tbsp. apple cider vinegar
- 1 Tbsp. toasted sesame oil
- 2 Tbsp. extra-virgin olive oil

**Salad**

- 2 ripe, juicy peaches
- 2 handfuls cherry tomatoes, such as Kumato, halved
- 2 large handfuls torn summer salad leaves, such as purslane, Castelfranco radicchio, arugula, and dandelion leaves
- 7 oz/200g halloumi cheese, drained and coarsely shredded
- Sea salt flakes
- Something crunchy: dukkah (page 18) or toasted hazelnuts
- Crisp seeded lavash or soft Persian flatbread, for serving

Mix all the dressing ingredients together and set aside.

Halve the peaches and remove the pits. Either coarsely chop the peaches, or tear and lightly squeeze into a mixing bowl. Add the tomatoes, then add the dressing, stir, and leave for 5 minutes.

Wash and spin-dry the salad leaves. Toss into the peach mixture, then add the shredded halloumi cheese, toss once more, and taste to see if salt is needed.

Transfer the salad to a serving bowl and sprinkle with the dukkah. Serve with lavash or flatbread to soak up all the delicious juices.

# Macerated Heirloom Tomatoes

A very simple recipe of macerating sliced heirloom tomatoes with extra-virgin olive oil, chiles, and herbs. It's the perfect serving partner for all creamy cheeses from triple-cream cheese, to blue cheese or goat cheese.

**SERVES 4**

3 large heirloom tomatoes, choose different colors

3 handfuls mixed cherry tomatoes, halved

Enough extra-virgin olive oil, for covering

1 to 2 dried red chiles, kept whole, or 1 tsp. hot pepper flakes

2 rosemary, oregano, or marjoram sprigs

Crusty sourdough, toasted pita bread, or thin crispy flatbread

Any of these cheeses: La Tur, creamy goat cheese, Roquefort, Gorgonzola, Point Reyes blue cheese, creamy feta in oil

A crunchy herb and chili mixture: za'atar, nutty dukkah (page 18), "Italian" chili herb blend or ground black pepper

Slice the tomatoes into ¼-inch-/ 5mm-thick slices. Place all tomatoes in a resealable, shallow container that will allow all the tomatoes to sit in a single-ish layer, and pour over the olive oil to cover. Add the chiles and herb of your choice. Cover and let stand overnight in the refrigerator or for at least 4 hours at room temperature. These tomatoes can be kept for up to three days.

Use the tomatoes accordingly, either for one sitting sharing with friends, or to prepare a bruschetta-style meal for yourself.

To serve, spread or crumble the cheese on the bread of your choice. Top with tomato, za'atar or dukkah or even, an "Italian" Calabrian chili crisp, or a sprinkle of black pepper.

# Watermelon, Heirloom Tomato, and Feta Salad

This summer salad is a mix of refreshing watermelon, heirloom tomatoes, cucumbers, arugula, and fresh herbs, which are all brought together with a rich salty feta. Serve big as a single-course salad. When I'm feeling a little extra indulgent, I splash out on feta marinated in extra-virgin olive oil.

**SERVES 2**

1 small watermelon wedge, about 12oz/350g, cut into big chunks

2 Persian cucumbers, coarsely cut into large pieces

1 large heirloom tomato of your choice, cut into large chunks

## Dressing

2 Tbsp. sherry or apple cider vinegar

1 tsp. chili sesame oil

3 Tbsp. extra-virgin olive oil

## Salad

2 big handfuls arugula, purslane, or torn radicchio leaves

1 big handful mint sprigs

1 handful flat-leaf parsley sprigs

7 oz/200g fresh feta or feta marinated in olive oil

Sea salt flakes and black pepper

1 red onion, thinly shaved and soaked in ice-cold water for 10 minutes, drained

Something crunchy: sesame crackers or pita chips, for serving

Place the watermelon, cucumbers, and tomato in a large bowl.

Mix all the dressing ingredients together and pour over the watermelon mixture. Let stand for 10 minutes.

Wash and spin-dry the salad leaves and herbs. Toss into the melon and tomato and mix just before serving.

Add the feta and lightly toss once more. Season with black pepper, taste, and add salt, if needed, but the feta might be enough. Sprinkle over the drained red onions and serve with seeded crackers.

# Burrata with Spicy Fresh Green Juice

One usually shares the burrata appetizer in a restaurant, but I like it to myself, so when I'm at home I make my own version of burrata combos, and that's my meal with crusty sourdough or crisp bread. The spicy fresh green juice is actually inspired by the Mexican aguachile.

**SERVES 2**

1 cup/125g frozen peas, thawed in cold water for 10 minutes

1 English cucumber, trimmed and cut into large chunks

1 jalapeño

1 cup/250ml store-bought dashi broth, chilled

1 small handful each of dill and flat-leaf parsley sprigs

Juice of 1 lemon

Sea salt flakes and black pepper

2 (4oz/115g) burrata, drained

Avocado or extra-virgin olive oil, for drizzling

Edible flowers, wood sorrel, dill sprigs, or pea tendrils, for garnishing

Crusty sourdough bread, for serving

Drain the peas and place in a Vitamix or blender with the cucumber, jalapeño, dashi broth, and herbs. Process for 3 minutes, or until very smooth and liquid.

Strain through a fine strainer, discarding the pulp. Gradually add and taste the amount of lemon juice needed. Season with salt and pepper. Chill the fresh juice until required.

When ready to serve, divide the juice between two serving bowls, place a burrata in the center of each, and just cut open a tiny bit. Drizzle with avocado oil and garnish with edible flowers or pea tendrils, if available. Serve with crusty bread.

**FLAVOR TIP**
You can find dashi in Japanese food stores. To make your own, mix 1 tsp. bonito flakes, 1 cup/250ml cold water, and a drop seasoned rice vinegar together. Let stand for 30 minutes, then strain to use.

# Melon Halloumi Fattoush

Fattoush is a traditional Middle Eastern salad flavored with lots of herbs, sumac, and Aleppo pepper, often with crunchy bread or crackers mixed in. In the summer, I replace the cucumber with a fragrant green honeydew, Galia, or yellow melon. I also turn it into a main course by adding shredded halloumi.

**SERVES 4**

## Dressing

1 Tbsp. sumac

½ to 1 tsp. Aleppo pepper

Juice of 1 lemon

2 garlic cloves, ideally grated on a microplane

6 Tbsp. extra-virgin olive oil

Sea salt flakes and black pepper

## Salad

1 small green melon, seeded and cut into 1-inch/2.5cm chunks

1 large heirloom tomato, cut into large pieces

2 handfuls coarsely chopped dandelion leaves, or young arugula

½ small head radicchio, torn into 1-inch/2.5cm pieces

2 handfuls mixed mint, cilantro, and flat-leaf parsley sprigs, keeping the sprigs big

2 small shallots, thinly sliced and soaked in ice-cold water for 10 minutes, drained

8 oz/225g halloumi, coarsely shredded and crumbled

Something crunchy: toasted pita chips, sesame crackers, or za'atar pita chips

Make the dressing by mixing the sumac, Aleppo pepper, lemon juice, and garlic together. Start to whisk in the olive oil until thick. You might not want to add all the oil if it seems thick enough for you. Season to taste.

Place the melon and tomatoes in a large serving bowl and add half the dressing. Let stand for 10 minutes. Add the salad leaves and herbs, toss a little more, and add the shallots, halloumi, and a little more dressing. Toss.

Just before serving, add the pita chips or crackers, toss, then serve with the remaining dressing.

**QUICK SWAP**
If you don't feel like making the dressing, substitute with 1 to 2 Tbsp. pomegranate molasses and 4 Tbsp. extra-virgin olive oil.

# Ricotta Salata with Persimmons

The salty ricotta salata in this dish complements the sweet winter seasonal persimmons and robust peppery radicchio. The Fuyu persimmon, the squatter-looking variety, has a good crunch to it and is great for salads as it always guarantees a good flavor. December to February are the ideal months to bring perfect persimmon sunshine and flavor to all winter salads.

**SERVES 2**

1 small head radicchio, torn into bite-size pieces

2 crunchy persimmons, thinly sliced

1 chunk of ricotta salata, thinly sliced

3 big splashes extra-virgin olive oil

2 Tbsp. red wine or sherry vinegar

1 pinch of hot pepper flakes

1 handful roasted almonds, coarsely chopped

Sea salt flakes and black pepper

Protein options: marinated goat cheese in olive oil, sliced fennel salami, or 2 pieces quartered rotisserie chicken, for serving

Crusty sesame sourdough bread, for serving

Scatter the radicchio on a platter or two individual plates. Randomly add the persimmons and sliced ricotta. Splash on the olive oil and vinegar.

Sprinkle with hot pepper flakes and almonds. Taste and season with salt (probably not needed) and black pepper. Serve with marinated goat cheese, and crusty bread.

# The Savory Sandwich Cake

This is quite the extravaganza, but a fun showstopper. The recipe is a little unexpected for my style of cooking, but friends love it and feel that I have gone the extra mile for them. The choice of bread is up to you, but for me, the Japanese milk bread is perfect, as the shape is always a big square, and there is still plenty of bread left over when the crusts are removed.

**EACH SANDWICH SERVES 2**

### Bread

4 slices milk bread or white sliced sandwich bread

Cultured butter, softened, for spreading

Sea salt flakes and black pepper

### Filling

Ham; cucumber ribbons mixed with chives, parsley, or micro shiso or cilantro leaves and lemon rind; chopped cooked shrimp mixed with Spicy Mayo (page 57)

### Cream cheese

4 Tbsp. cream cheese seasoned with lemon juice or a little pickle juice of your choice, and 1 to 2 pinches of salt

### Garnishes

Sticks of gherkins or cornichons; dill or fennel fronds; fish roe or radishes, shaved, and soaked in ice-cold water; edible flowers; 2 whole peeled shrimp with tails intact; cucumber ribbons

To assemble, spread a first slice of bread with butter and season with salt and pepper. Top with thinly sliced ham of your choice, piling it up to about 1 inch/2.5cm thick.

Spread a second piece of bread with butter on both sides. Place on the ham, and top with the cucumber filling.

Take a third piece of bread and spread with butter. Place buttered-side down on the cucumbers. Top with chopped shrimp.

Place the final layer of bread on the shrimp and press down slightly. I like to help the situation a little, so I put four toothpicks into the sandwich cake to hold it all in place—just remember where they are and warn friends if you don't take them out.

Use a good, serrated knife, or I like to use an electric knife for a clean cut every time, and slice the crusts from all sides of the sandwich.

Spread the cream cheese mixture on top and sides of the sandwich, then chill for at least 30 minutes, or up to 3 hours until needed.

Just before serving, cut the sandwich in half, either into two rectangles or triangles. Place each onto a serving plate and garnish.

For the garnish, stack sticks of gherkins or cornichons on one side of the sandwich half, interspersing with dill or fennel fronds to create a cornichon flower! Place fish roe to the side of that with some edible flowers. Add a whole shrimp, a ribbon or two of cucumber, some more pickles or shaved radishes, and another sprinkling of flowers. It's up to you. Serve with a lemon wedge and knife!

# Modern Cheese on Toast

This is not the usual melting grilled cheese, but the modern version of a creamy luxurious soft cheese topped with some punch.

## Building Blocks

### Bread
Sourdough, rye, mixed seeded gluten-free breads, crackers, seeded crackers.

### Cheese
Vacherin Mont d'Or, ricotta, Humboldt Fog (ash goat cheese), cream cheese, cottage cheese, burrata, mascarpone, blue cheeses such as Point Reyes, Epoisses (red rind).

### Pickles
Ready-made (page 21) or store-bought—radishes, onions, cucumbers, chopped vegetables.

### Drizzle of
Extra-virgin olive oil, honey, chili honey, pomegranate molasses, or date molasses.

### Crunch
Toasted chopped nuts, such as almonds, hazelnuts, pistachios, walnuts, pecans, pumpkin seeds, sunflower seeds; crunchy spice mixes like dukkah, salsa seca, chili crisp; and/or chopped chocolate.

### Final Touch
Microgreens, such as cilantro, amaranth, shiso, radish; scallion ribbons; flower and vegetables petals; sliced cherry tomatoes; shaved radishes; red currants, raspberries, and black currants; thinly shaved apples, pears, and persimmons.

## Exceptional Combos (Opposite, clockwise from top left)

| Vacherin Mont d'Or | Creamy Gorgonzola | Humboldt Fog | Mascarpone |
|---|---|---|---|
| Milk or white bread | Sourdough toast | Danish rye seeded bread | Sweet olive oil crisp cracker |
| Vacherin Mont d'Or | Gorgonzola Dolce | Ash goat cheese/ Humboldt Fog | Mascarpone |
| Torn figs | Mixed shaved pickles, such as yellow beets and watermelon radishes | Quince jelly | Shaved Asian pears |
| Drizzle of honey or extra-virgin olive oil | Pistachios | Splash of sherry vinegar | Szechuan chili crisp |
| Chocolate and hazelnuts | Chili honey | Crispy onions | Amaranth or sunflower microgreens |

# Main Course Cheese Plates

The cheese plate has become the ultimate "grazing" dinner. It hones in on a single cheese with its accoutrements, plus a glass of wine, crispbreads, crackers, or a hunk of bread.

### White Cheese Plate

Fresh ricotta, or feta, or goat cheese

Shaved salad of zucchini, sugar snaps, fresh peas, and/or fresh fava beans, mint sprigs, and pansies

Drizzle with extra-virgin olive oil and pomegranate molasses

Chilled white wine like a simple Pinot Grigio or Sorriso

**Parmesan Plate**

Aged Parmesan
or Pecorino cheese

Thinly sliced pears
or peaches
(depending on season)

Orange marmalade

Red Belgian endive

Roasted almonds

Crispbread/crackers

Chilled red wine

## Comte or Gouda Plate

Semi-soft Comte
or Gouda

Tangy green apples

Celery or fennel sticks

Sweet gold cherry tomatoes

Pickled beets or
vegetables (page 21)

Whole wheat salty crackers

Chilled orange wine

## Creamy
## Goat Cheese Plate

**Humboldt Fog,
or bucheron**

**Shaved fennel,
tender new-season
asparagus,
little gem lettuce**

**Sliced persimmons**

**Blackberries**

**Marcona almonds**

**Chilled light rosé wine**

A light rosé wine
made from Gamay
2020 is very good.

# A Spoonful of Cheese!

All you want is a tiny bite of something to fill that gap. Sometimes mine might just be anchovy in spicy oil, but recently, I've taken to eating sweet fig jam and a slither of feta cheese ... what's your quick fix?

**Ricotta with buckwheat or chestnut honey**

**Fig jam (spicy or sweet) with a slice of feta**

**Mascarpone, Stracciatella, or ricotta with passion fruit**

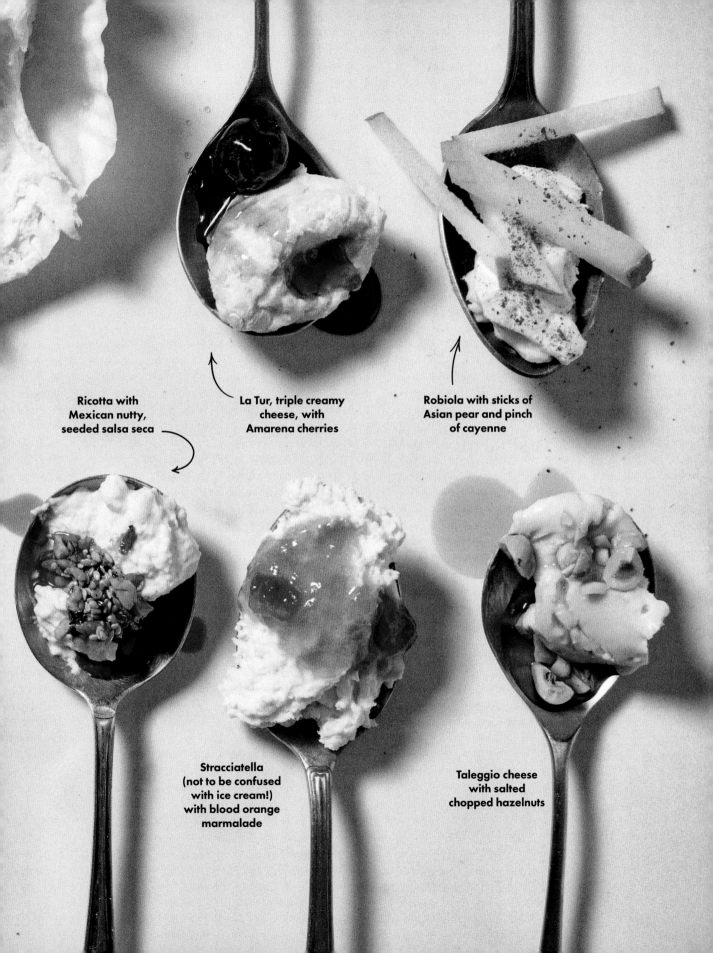

**Ricotta with Mexican nutty, seeded salsa seca**

**La Tur, triple creamy cheese, with Amarena cherries**

**Robiola with sticks of Asian pear and pinch of cayenne**

**Stracciatella (not to be confused with ice cream!) with blood orange marmalade**

**Taleggio cheese with salted chopped hazelnuts**

# The Breakfast Cheese Board

What kind of cheese do you want to eat for breakfast? Soft and creamy to allow you to spread it on toast? Mellow or tart with hints of sweet? You can then decide on your other additions of cured fish and pickles.

## Building Blocks

### Cheeses
Choose one to two cheeses and possibly a schmear of butter.

### Non-ripened, spreadable cheeses:
• Farmer's cheese—similar to cottage cheese, but the whey is pressed from the curds, rather than just draining; this way the texture is creamier than cottage cheese. It has a tart, slightly acid taste, depending on whether it's made from cow, sheep, or goat milk.

• Ricotta—this is a by-product of Parmesan cheese-making (hence re-cooked!). It uses the whey from sheep, cow, goat, or buffalo. The flavor is mellow and creamy, but can also be gamey depending on the producer.

• Cream cheese—this is cream mixed with lactic acid to help with the coagulation. Once the cream is curdled, it's processed to a creamy texture. The flavor is slightly sweet with a mild acidic taste.

• Mascarpone—a sweet Italian cheese where the cream is curdled with lactic acid. It is sweet in flavor with a very high fat content. Ideally served with fruit and more sweets at the breakfast table for pure indulgence.

• Mozzarella—a fresh mozzarella, made from cow or buffalo milk, will have that mellow and tender tanginess. Its texture is not spreadable, but it can have a place on the breakfast cheese board.

### Ripened soft cheese from the "bloomy-rind family":
• For the breakfast cheese board, stick with the more mellow, buttery tasting Bries, sometimes a little salty, but never sweet. This cheese will have been ripened from as little as two weeks to twenty-four weeks. Varieties such as Brie Fermier, French double crème, a Camembert de Normandie, crottin—Bijou creamery; something a touch riper would be the Saint André, Brillat-Savarin, La Tur, and the slightly blue Humboldt Fog.

### Breads
Seeded rye, crackers, rolls—sourdough, brioche, bagel—flatbread, fruit bread such as raisin and pecan.

### Extra breakfast protein
Smoked fish, ham, and avocado—not quite a protein I know, but a modern breakfast essential for richness.

### Sharpness
Pickles like capers, caper berries, gherkins, half sour pickles, pickled green tomatoes.

### Fresh
Tomatoes, fresh cucumbers, sharp/tart fruit, and mellow/sweet fruit, such as apples, pears, and oranges.

**Opposite, clockwise from top left: St Stephen's Brillat-Savarin, ricotta, classic cream cheese, mascarpone, mozzarella, farmer's cheese.**

# Two Breakfast Cheese Boards

## Cream Cheese and Brillat-Savarin Board

Dollop **3** heaping spoonfuls of cream cheese, in a small bowl, and schmear the top with the back of a spoon. Place on a board. Add **8** thin slices of smoked salmon or lox, **1 large**, sliced heirloom tomato, and a small round triple-cream cheese (St Stephen's Brillat-Savarin or Saint André). Peel and remove the rind from **2 blood oranges** and slice into disks. Place in a bowl with a handful of **blackberries**. Finish with a handful of **microgreens**. Serve with **sourdough bread** and/or **crackers**. Serves 2 to 4

## Goat Cheese and Mozzarella Board

Coat **6 disks of goat cheese** with **furikake** and place on a platter. Flake a **4oz/110g piece of hot-smoked salmon or trout** (discarding the skin) and add to the platter. Slice **1 Persian cucumber** into ribbons. Add to the platter and top with ½ **avocado**, diced, and a handful of **caper berries**. In a bowl, add **1 buffalo mozzarella** cut into four, and spoon over **1 passion fruit** and a drizzle of **extra-virgin olive oil**, and place on the platter. Serve with **multigrain bread** and **olive oil crackers**. Serves 2 to 3

# The Cheese Board for a Dinner Crowd

As much as I don't like rules for food, you can have a few when putting a cheese board together. However, I came up with some questions: do I create a board of three cheeses where it's a different milk (cow, goat, sheep)? Or do I go by texture (soft, semi-hard, hard, blue)? Myself, I often go with the latter.

## Building Blocks

### How many people are you serving?
- Eight people: three cheeses (each about 12oz to 1lb/350 to 450g).
- 12 to 16 people: five cheeses (blocks varying from 5oz/140g, 12oz/350g, two 8oz/225g, 1lb/450g). Allow the cheeses to be different sizes.

### Cheeses
- Soft—if you like Brie, choose cheeses like Moses Sleeper, Winnimere, then move onto the washed rind Humboldt Fog or Vacherin Mont d'Or. In this section, I would hold off from the white cheeses like burrata, mozzarella, and feta, as they are very much stand-alone cheeses.
- Semi hard—cheddar (Neal's Yard Montgomery is unbeatable), Fontina Val d'Aosta or Fontina Alpina, Havarti, Manchego semi curado.
- Hard—aged Parmesan, Grana Padano, aged goat or sheep Gouda.
- Blue—Point Reyes, a creamy Gorgonzola, Roquefort Papillon, Cashel blue.

### Breads and Crackers
Sourdough, herbed bread (like rosemary focaccia), crackers (taralli, salt sourdough crackers, herbed crackers), and flatbreads like lavash.

### Acid
Pickles, such as capers, caper berries, gherkins, marinated green olives; pickled vegetables (page 21), dried sour cherries, dried apricots, dried pineapple, and dried persimmons.

### Fresh
Fruits and vegetables—apples, pears, Asian pears (my favorite because of their fragrance), apricots, peaches and nectarines, fresh raspberries, grapes—red and green—wedges of yellow, orange, and green melon (described by color, but all are fragrant and sweet in season).

### Additional Touch
Caramel chocolate, dark chocolate, chocolate-coated almonds, herb flowers from chive flowers to peppery nasturtiums and marigold petals.

Opposite, clockwise from center: Mature Parmesan; sliced dried persimmons; rich Gorgonzola Dolce; pickled okra; taralli crackers; chopped chocolate; triple cream Brillat-Savarin sprinkled with marigold petals; cantaloupe melon; mature cheddar; fresh apricots.

# Something to Finish

*Shakes, Sundaes, and Bites*

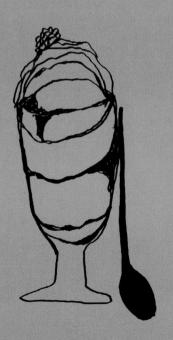

I have a good sweet tooth and love most things sweet, especially Cadbury's chocolate. Traditionally, one was laughed at if they had a "weird" liking for a taste combo—salted chips or pickles with ice cream, or anchovies with anything sweet. This chapter dives into the cupboard, freezer, or the local cuisine in your area (for me, in London, it's Turkish, so I can get the best baklavas ever) to see what there is, and how you can make the best pairings possible.

Which ingredients make an easy, comforting bite to end a meal? Semi-dried fruit (dates and persimmons); sweet preserves and condiments (jams, fruits in syrup), cookies and ice cream—yes all normal, but then start to combine these with snacking salty foods and many an interesting concoction is assembled.

This chapter might be a bite of something sweet, or even a savory taste that will finish off a meal. Or it's a middle-of-the-day treat that will put a skip in your step.

### PREP TIPS

- Shredded halva is a Middle Eastern and Persian cotton candy. The name to look for is Pismaniye.

- Frozen berries make instant sorbets when you need an easy pick-me-up.

- If you are overloaded with ripe bananas, thinly slice, and place on a sheet pan lined with plastic wrap. Freeze until solid then repack in a resealable container. Use to make shakes, and simple quick "frozen banana cream" with a drizzle of maple syrup.

Clockwise from top left: Frozen bananas; the Cherry and Lychee Salad (page 207); Persian cotton candy; lining the glasses with pomegranate molasses; frozen mixed berries.

# Shakes with Oomph

These shakes all rely on having frozen fruit in the freezer, especially frozen bananas, which come in very handy (see tip on page 198). I love shakes and these Middle Eastern flavors really give them some character.

**EACH RECIPE SERVES 2**

## Halva and Pomegranate

Add **1 cup/140g frozen mango chunks** to a Vitamix and add **1 Tbsp. pomegranate molasses**, about **1-in/2.5cm piece of halva**, **8 slices of frozen banana**, **1 cup/250ml milk of choice**, and **6 to 8 ice cubes**. Whizz until smooth. Pour **1 Tbsp. pomegranate molasses** into two serving glasses. Use a pastry brush to make strokes of syrup up the sides of the glasses. Pour in the shake and top with a chunk of **shredded halva**, opened out with your fingers. Drizzle with pomegranate molasses and a sprinkling of **pistachios**.

How to serve—spoon or thick straw or both.

## Ginger, Molasses, and Banana

One of my favorite cookies happens to be a soft and chewy ginger molasses cookie. Break up **1 cookie**, place in a Vitamix, and whizz until very crumbly. Add **8 slices of frozen banana** with 1 cup/250ml milk of your choice, and **6 to 8 ice cubes**. Whizz until smooth. Pour about **1 Tbsp. blackstrap molasses** into two tall serving glasses and use a pastry brush to make strokes up the sides of the glasses. Pour in the shake and top with **whipped cream**, a drizzle of molasses, and a couple of cookie quarters per glass.

## Brownie and Banana

Add **2 squares of brownie or 2 Oreos** to a Vitamix or blender and whizz to form crumbs. Set aside
2 Tbsp. crumbs. Add **8 slices of frozen banana, 1 cup/250ml milk of your choice, and 6 to 8 ice cubes**
to the Vitamix with the remaining crumbs and whizz until super smooth. Drizzle two tall glasses with 1 Tbsp.
each of **chocolate sauce or syrup** and brush halfway up the sides of the glasses. Pour in the shake, add a
dollop or two of **whipped cream or cool whip,** and finish with the reserved brownie crumbs.

## Tahini and Date

Add **8 slices of frozen banana** to the Vitamix or blender, **1 cup/250ml oat or cashew milk**, **2 pitted, Medjool dates**, **6 to 8 ice cubes**, and **2 Tbsp. tahini paste** (mixed well in the jar before scooping out). Whizz everything together until smooth. Take 2 tall glasses and drizzle spirals inside of the glass with **date syrup** and quickly pour in the shake. Top with a small bundle of **shredded halva**, pulling the shreds apart slightly, drizzle a little more date syrup. So naughty but perfect.

# Platter of Ice Cream and Fixings

What's in the pantry to go with ice cream? Salty tortilla chips or salt and vinegar chips, cherries in syrup (Italian Amarena cherries), extra-virgin olive oil, or even the Mexican spice mixture Tajin.

**SERVES 4 TO 6**

## Building Blocks

### Ice Cream
2 to 3 pints/450ml different ice cream, such as vanilla, caramel, chocolate chip; or sorbets, such as chocolate, blood orange or mango.

### The Fixings
Crunchy and salty—tortilla chips, salt and vinegar chips, crushed pretzel pieces, salty popcorn, salted peanuts.

Sweet syrupy preserves —Italian Amarena cherries, Turkish rose jam, pomegranate molasses, blackstrap molasses, chocolate sauce, chili honey.

Spice—black peppercorns, Mexican Tajin, Sichuan chili crisp, salsa seca.

Sweet fruit—overripe peaches, nectarines, apricots, blood oranges, cara cara oranges, fresh grated coconut.

### Assemble
Place the actual ice-cream containers into large bowls filled with ice.

Provide several ice-cream scoops, then place all the fixings in serving bowls and let friends and family make their own cups or glasses of ice-cream combos.

## Exceptional Combos (Opposite, clockwise from top left)

| Sweet and Salty | Touch of Citrus | Spicy Hot | Floral and Fragrant |
|---|---|---|---|
| Amarena cherries and syrup | Blood oranges | Salted roasted peanuts | Ripe, juicy peaches |
| Salty crushed chips | Tajin | Chili honey | Extra-virgin olive oil |
| Vanilla ice cream | Mango sorbet | Vanilla ice cream | Chocolate sorbet |

# Quick Fruit Desserts

I have enjoyed these clever yet simple desserts in both Chicago and New York and they taste just as good recreated at home.

**EACH RECIPE SERVES 4**

Use either walnut or pistachio baklava.

## Berry Sorbet and Baklava

Put **2 cups/325g frozen berries** in a food processor with **1 cup/250ml Greek yogurt** and **1 to 2 Tbsp. maple syrup** and process for 2 to 3 minutes until super smooth. Coarsely chop **2 small squares of baklava**. To assemble, put 2 Tbsp. sorbet into the base of four serving bowls and sprinkle with half the baklava. Add the remaining sorbet, finishing with the baklava. Serve immediately or freeze until required.

## Cherry and Lychee Salad

Drain **1 can or jar (15oz/425g) pitted cherries in syrup** (not thick pie filling) and place in a bowl.
Drain **1 can (15oz/425g) lychees in syrup** and add to the cherries. Stir to mix. Pour in **1 cup/250ml
evaporated milk** of your choice—be it oat, cow, or coconut. Chop **2oz/50g sesame crunch bar** and
sprinkle over the dessert. You can use chopped pistachios or grated dark chocolate, if liked.

Opposite: Chopping sesame bars to sprinkle over the Cherry and Lychee Salad (page 207). This page: Baklava from a Middle Eastern pastry store.

# Loaded Cookie Platter

Build the platter with a few cookies of choice, add the fixings, and off you go for a fun movie night or simply a dessert that took no time to put together.

---

## Building Blocks

### Cookies
Choose jumbo cookies—chocolate chunk, triple chocolate, ginger molasses, oatmeal and raisin, peanut butter, walnut and chocolate.

### Creamy
Ice cream, whipped cream, mascarpone, ricotta cheese, cream cheese, berry sorbet, nut butter.

### Fruit
Sliced bananas, juicy berries, stone fruit.

### Sprinkles or Something Special
Chopped candied oranges, chopped pistachios, popcorn, maraschino cherry, shredded halva, chopped chocolate, pomegranates.

### Sauce
Chocolate sauce, raspberry sauce, pomegranate molasses, date molasses, honey.

---

## Exceptional Combos (Opposite, clockwise from top left)

| Double Chocolate Cookie | Ginger Molasses Cookie | Chocolate Chunk Cookie | Oatmeal and Raisin Cookie |
|---|---|---|---|
| Pistachio butter | Mascarpone | Vanilla ice cream | Ricotta |
| Crushed raspberries | Crushed blackberries | Bananas | Raspberries |
| Drizzle of honey | Drizzle of honey | Raspberries | Pomegranate molasses |
| Whipped cream | | Chopped peanuts | |
| Chopped pistachios | | Popcorn | |
| | | Chocolate sauce | |

# Bites to be Savored

Sweet, ripe fruits teamed with a savory-ish pinch of spice or filled with a creamy cheese elevates them to something special. Serve for easy after-dinner bites or a pick-me-up snack.

**Blood oranges and pink Himalayan or black salt**

**Ripe strawberries and pomegranate powder**

**Medjool dates, feta, tahini, and extra-virgin olive oil**

**Medjool dates, Gorgonzola, and walnuts**

Medjool dates, ricotta, almonds, and ground cinnamon

Medjool dates, mascarpone, and pomegranate molasses

Cantaloupe melon and Indian Masala chaat spice

Watermelon and Tajin spice

Medjool dates and halva

Ripe peaches and sesame dukkah

Medjool dates, goat cheese, and pistachios

# Suggested Menus

*For Two, Three, Six, or a Crowd*

# Menu Scenarios

The Greek in me loves to share and socialize around food. It's no problem for me to have friends drop in to say hello and then to stay for an easy dinner. These no-cook recipes and a well-stocked pantry means I'm ready for any impromptu "party." Even if you just have a cup of tea or coffee with me, I will offer some Medjool dates, chocolate-coated almonds, and a sliced pear.

## Brunch for Two

**Goat cheese and Mozzarella Board, page 193**

Or Cream Cheese and Brillat-Savarin Board, page 192

Or Lox Grain Bowl, page 78

Or Modern Cheese on Toast, page 182

**Choice of stuffed dates, page 212**

Or an indulgent shake, such as Halva and Pomegranate, page 200

## Brunch for a Crowd

**Smoked Fish Board For a Crowd, page 90**

Or Lobster, Shrimp, and Crab Brioche Rolls, page 76

**With Melon Halloumi Fattoush, page 176**

**Cherry and Lychee Salad, page 207**

## Lunch for Two

Turkey Tonnato, page 123

    Or Tuna and Tomato Salad, page 64

    Or The Savory Sandwich Cake, page 180

Cherry and Lychee Salad, page 207

    Or Comte or Gouda Plate, page 186

## Lunch for a Crowd

Springtime Fattoush with Shrimp, page 97

The Green Goddess Chicken Salad Wedge, page 38

Fall Salad with Prosciutto, page 106

Loaded Cookie Platter, page 210

## Friends Popping Over

White Bean, Pickled Beets, and Radicchio Salad, page 138

    Or Vietnamese Salad with Chicken, page 52

    Or Wild Marinated Mushrooms and Chicken Bruschetta, page 46

    Or Tinned Sardine Platter or Mackerel Plate, pages 68 and 69

Platter of Ice Cream and Fixings, page 204

    Or A spoonful of cheese or two, page 188

## Family Dinner + Extra Kids

Family Taco Salad Platter, page 42

    Or Platter of Lentils, Salami, and Oranges, page 116

Loaded Cookie Platter, page 210

    Or Platter of Ice Cream and Fixings, page 204

    Or Cherry and Lychee Salad, page 207

## Game Night for Six

Deluxe Board (tinned fish), page 71

And Italian Cold Cuts with Marinated Artichokes, page 112

    Or Charcuterie on a Stick, page 132—pick a selection of three

    Or The Cheese Board For a Dinner Crowd, page 194

Mexican Shrimp Cocktail, page 75

    Or Simple Ceviche, page 85

Platter of Ice Cream and Fixings, page 204

    Or Loaded Cookie Platter, page 210

## Sports on the Telly

Muffuletta, page 124

And Giardiniera Chicken Baguette, page 46

    Or Lobster, Shrimp, and Crab Brioche Rolls, page 76

The Dip Platter, page 146

    Or Store-Bought Hummus All Dressed-Up, page 150

Loaded Cookie Platter, page 210

    Or Platter of Ice Cream and Fixings, page 204

# Acknowledgments

I'd like to equally and enthusiastically thank everyone involved in making this book ... and now I will break it down below!

To Catie Ziller, my publisher, who has always had faith in me and my book ideas. Taking us all the way back to 2000, even when I was 2 hours late for our first meeting! We did have a great meeting and a bestseller at the beginning of a coffee craze in 2001.

Thank you to Michele Outland, creative director, and designer for this book. You really did read between the lines to create such a simple-to-follow cookbook, making room for the brilliant big pictures. Which brings me to photographer Alex Lau. Thank you, Alex, for taking such beautiful pictures of food; I know our schedule was crazy. I have loved collaborating with both Michele and Alex, I met them both very early on in their careers and now I am lucky they still want to work with me, even though they are at the very top of our industry.

Thank you to Nidia and Nico at PropLink LA for the use of the perfect props and surfaces; and to ARJ LA for the loan of the beautiful Korean ceramics.

Big shout out to artist Heather Chontos for her drawings and interpretations of the chapter openers. I love them, thank you.

To my three assistants who worked with me at different times on the shoots of this cookbook—Sophia Green, Matteo Connolly, and Chantael Takeuchi. You are all excellent cooks with brilliant points of view, and I really do enjoy cooking with all of you.

To my many good friends, Ellen Morrissey, Michelle Fiordaliso, Wren Arthur, Claudia Kalindjian, and Charlie Peters, who read parts of this book, my intro especially, the covers, the ideas. Consulting with all of you, was an important part of the process for me. I loved your take on food, no-cook and lots more ... especially as I know how much you all enjoy cooking. I also roped in two of my nieces, Nicole and Josie Theodorou to help; thank you both. And also, to my friends who I have shared many meals with, and who have inspired me to constantly search for delicious flavors and combinations.

To my Greek Cypriot family, my mum and her sisters, who are full of inspiration for food and juggling life to make it perfect for everyone around them. They still do even into their seventies and eighties—they really are remarkable.

X Susie

Hardie Grant North America
2912 Telegraph Ave
Berkeley, CA 94705
hardiegrantusa.com

Published in the United States by
Hardie Grant North America, an imprint
of Hardie Grant Publishing Pty Ltd.

Library of Congress Cataloging-in-
Publication Data is available upon request
ISBN: 9781958417553
ISBN: 9781958417560 (eBook)

Acquiring Editor: Catie Ziller
Creative Director and Designer:
 Michele Outland
Photographer: Alex Lau
Food and Prop Styling: Susie Theodorou
Assistants: Sophia Green,
 Matteo Connolly, Chantael Takeuchi
Drawings: Heather Chontos
Copy Editor: Kathy Steer

Printed in China

FIRST EDITION

Hardie Grant

NORTH AMERICA